COMBAT AIRCRAFT

115 Fw 200 CONDOR UNITS OF WORLD WAR 2

SERIES EDITOR TONY HOLMES

115

**COMBAT
AIRCRAFT**

Chris Goss

Fw 200 CONDOR UNITS
OF WORLD WAR 2

OSPREY

PUBLISHING

First published in Great Britain in 2016 by Osprey Publishing
PO Box 883, Oxford, OX1 9PL, UK
1385 Broadway, 5th Floor, New York, NY 10018, USA

E-mail: info@ospreypublishing.com

Osprey Publishing, part of Bloomsbury Publishing Plc

A CIP catalogue record for this book is available from the British Library

ISBN: 978 1 4728 1267 4
PDF e-book ISBN: 978 1 4728 1268 1
e-Pub ISBN: 978 1 4728 1269 8

Edited by Tony Holmes and Philip Jarrett
Cover Artwork by Mark Postlethwaite
Aircraft Profiles by Chris Davey
Index by Zoe Ross
Originated by PDQ Digital Media Solutions, UK
Printed in China through World Print Ltd

16 17 18 19 20 10 9 8 7 6 5 4 3 2 1

Osprey Publishing supports the Woodland Trust, the UK's leading woodland
conservation charity. Between 2014 and 2018 our donations will be spent on their
Centenary Woods project in the UK.

www.ospreypublishing.com

Acknowledgements
The author would like to thank Andrew Bird, Justin Horgan, Tony Kearns,
Ed North, Tim Oliver, Günther Ott and Bernd Rauchbach for their assistance
with the compilation of this volume.

Front Cover
At 0205 hrs on 17 July 1941, Fw 200C-3
Wk-Nr 0063, coded F8+CL, of 3./KG 40
took off from Cognac, in France, on a
combined weather and armed
reconnaissance mission over the Atlantic.
At the controls were Oberleutnant Rudolf
Heindl, with second pilot Unteroffizier
Edgar Siegmund sat alongside him. The
rest of the crew consisted of Oberleutnant
Hans Jordens (radio operator), Unteroffizier
Carl Reichl (radio operator), Feldwebel
Hans Singer (flight engineer), Feldwebel
Walter Pflugbeil (observer) and
meteorologist Regierungs-Rat von Hartel.

Shortly after 0800 hrs, whilst flying at
just 50 ft above the sea, the Condor crew
spotted Convoy OB 346 sailing northwards
off the west coast of Ireland. They noted
that there were 36 freighters up to 10,000
brt, four destroyers and five frigates, as
well as a single Armstrong Whitworth
Whitley patrolling overhead. The latter,
Z6635/YG-Q of No 502 Sqn crewed by
Wg Cdr Don Shore (Captain), Flg Off Arthur
Brock, Plt Off John Macleod and
Sgts S Larmour and Basil Henson,
immediately turned towards the Condor
in order to protect the convoy.

In a running battle that lasted six
minutes, the Condor was hit in one of its
inner engines and 27-year-old Hans
Jordens was fatally wounded. However, the
German gunners were more accurate than
their RAF counterparts, hitting the
Whitley's cockpit and wounding Wg Cdr
Shore and two other crewmen. They also
started a fire amongst the aircraft's
'pyrotechnics' and damaged the starboard
engine. The Whitley turned away and the
Condor climbed into cloud and headed for
France. Four minutes later Z6635 began
to lose power from its starboard engine,
which then caught fire. Wg Cdr Shore
made the decision to ditch, after which
the crew quickly took to a dinghy that had
been punctured by bullets in the combat.
They were soon rescued by HMS
Westcott, however.

Wk-Nr 0063 landed without incident at
Brest at 1200 hrs. This aircraft was later
assigned to 7./KG 40 and recoded F8+BR,
only for it to suffer technical problems that
resulted in it ditching at Storsdahlsfjord,
off Norway, on 22 February 1942. The
remains of the aeroplane were recovered
in May 1999 and can now can be seen
under restoration at the *Deutsches
Technikmuseum* in Berlin *(Cover artwork
by Mark Postlethwaite)*

CONTENTS

CHAPTER ONE

TO WAR

Designed by Kurt Tank, Technical Director of the Focke-Wulf Flugzeugbau, as a four-engined airliner, the Fw 200 first flew in July 1937 with Tank himself at the controls. Once in production, the airliner's ability to fly passengers over long distances was quickly proven, with flights to Cairo in July 1938, then to New York the following month and Tokyo in November of that same year (although the aircraft on this last flight was lost in an accident off Manila on the return trip when two engines failed as it was landing). Such flights impressed Finnish, Danish and Brazilian national airlines. Indeed, aside from its use by *Deutsche Luft Hansa* (*DLH*), Danish airline *Det Danske Luftfartselskab* (*DDL*) and the Brazilian *Syndicato Condor* also acquired a handful of Fw 200s. Finally, the Japanese ordered five civil versions and one for military use.

The Fw 200 V1 prototype approaches New York City on 11 August 1938, the aircraft having taken 24 hours and 36 minutes to fly the 6371 km from Berlin. This flight was a major propaganda coup for *DLH*, the Third Reich and Focke-Wulf Flugzeugbau

Early in 1939, prompted by the Japanese need for a military variant, Kurt Tank began modifying the Fw 200B to perform the maritime reconnaissance role. The result was

The classic lines of *DLH* Fw 200A-0 D-ACVH, christened *GRENZMARK*. This aircraft subsequently became NK+NM and was assigned to the *FdF*

the Fw 200C, which was essentially similar to the Fw 200B-2 but with a dorsal turret, two guns in a ventral gondola, increased fuel capacity and floor-mounted cameras. By now the Luftwaffe had noticed the Fw 200's potential as a long-range reconnaissance aircraft capable of operating far out to sea, and, following completion of the first prototype (Fw 200 V10 Wk-Nr 0001, named *Hessen*), it ordered ten Fw 200C-0s to be built.

TO WAR

As a result of the power struggle between the Kriegsmarine and the Luftwaffe as to who would be in charge of maritime combat aircraft, in October 1939 *Reichsmarschall* Hermann Göring rejected the notion that aircraft assigned to the Kriegsmarine would be engaged in offensive missions. He stated that in future, reconnaissance of British coastal waters should be carried out by the Luftwaffe's X. *Fliegerkorps*, with all but six long-range-reconnaissance *Staffeln* and nine multipurpose mine *Staffeln* remaining with the Kriegsmarine for missions over the North Sea and its approaches. All other maritime units would transfer to X. *Fliegerkorps*. At about this time the Condor began to make an appearance in the frontline, and it would soon become synonymous with German maritime operations.

In September 1939 Hauptmann Edgar Petersen, formerly *Staffelkapitän* of 1. *Staffel* of *Kampfgeschwader* 51 (1./KG 51) and now serving with *General zur besonderen Verwendung der Luftflotte* 2, began championing the use of the Fw 200 for long-range maritime missions. As he stated after the war;

'I looked around for a suitable aeroplane in Germany. There was the [Junkers] Ju 90, but there were only two of these available and no production line had been set up. On the other hand, the Focke-Wulf company had four Fw 200s nearing completion, intended for delivery to Japan. I took these and a further six standard Fw 200 transports, and with these I set up my *Fernaufklärungsstaffel* at Bremen on 1 October 1939.'

In addition to the creation of Petersen's unit, another specialist formation, *Versuchsstelle für Höhenflug* (part of *Aufklärungsgruppe Oberbefehlshaber der Luftwaffe*, abbreviated as *Aufkl OBdL*), had been established at Berlin-Werder, and it was this unit that suffered the first military Condor accident when, on 23 November 1939, Fw 200 V10 experienced engine failure at Jever, in northern Germany, resulting in 50 per cent damage.

Formerly D-ARHU of *DLH*, the Fw 200 V-3 was originally named *Ostmark*. However, when it became 26+00 the Condor was renamed *Immelmann II* and assigned to the *FdF*

Petersen now began selecting and training crews, and in April 1940 the *Fernaufklärungsstaffel* was redesignated 1./KG 40, soon to be part of I./KG 40, and was in action over and around Norway from 10 April 1940 onwards. However, Condor numbers were still limited. For example, I./KG 40's strength on 10 May 1940 was just four aircraft, of which only two were serviceable.

The first Condor loss on an operational mission occurred during an evening reconnaissance of Narvik on 22 April 1940 when it is thought that Oberleutnant Karl-August Beckhaus and his crew were victims of weather or mechanical failure. On the same day a Condor being operated in the transport role by 4./*Kampfgeschwader zur besonderen Verwendung* 107 (4./KGzbV 107) crashed at Berlin-Staaken, killing Oberleutnant Alfred Henke and three crew. Just over a month later, on 25 May 1940, Oberleutnant Hellmuth Schöpke's crew became the first to be shot down by enemy aircraft when Flg Off Herman Grant-Ede of No 263 Sqn, flying a Gloster Gladiator, intercepted their Condor. It was forced to crash-land in the sea near Dyrøy Island, off the Norwegian coast, and Schopke and one of his crew were captured. A third crewman was killed and two more evaded. Grant-Ede had never seen a Condor before, and he thought his victim was a Ju 90 transporter. He filed two combat reports on the 25th, the first stating;

The first military Condor to suffer an incident was Fw 200 V10 Wk-Nr 0001 BS+AF. Originally coded D-ASHH and named *Hessen*, it was assigned to Oberstleutnant Theodor Rowehl's *Versuchsstelle für Höhenflug*, part of *Aufklärungsgruppe Oberbefehlshaber der Luftwaffe*. Converted to carry cameras, and with an increased fuel capacity, the aeroplane suffered engine failure on takeoff from Jever on 23 November 1939. It had been tasked with flying a reconnaissance mission to Iceland and the Faroe Islands. Flugkapitän Martin Königs and his crew were uninjured but the aircraft suffered 50 per cent damage

'Red Section took off at 0905 for a defensive patrol of Harstad-Skaanland area. Anti-aircraft bursts showed position of enemy aircraft, which was pursued and jettisoned its bombs four miles southeast of Lemminvaer. Eight large bombs were observed to drop from outer engines. Speed 250 to 350 mph, attack No 1 used and at 1000 yards two short bursts fired, buy no hits. Enemy aircraft using tracer from single gun on top rear turret. Enemy aircraft was low-wing four-engined monoplane with dirty green camouflage and single rudder. Enemy aircraft dived to sea level and escaped seawards due to superior speed.'

Even though Grant-Ede was credited with shooting this aircraft down, by his own admission he fired only twice, did not hit it and the 'four-engined monoplane' got away. The second combat some 50 minutes later was more conclusive;

'On return from previous combat, AA [anti-aircraft] fire observed over Harstad at about 1025 hrs. Enemy

Veteran pilot Edgar Petersen was the first to champion the use of the Fw 200 for long-range maritime missions. He was duly given permission to set up a *Fernaufklärungsstaffel*, equipped with Fw 200s, at Bremen on 1 October 1939

Originally built as an Fw 200B-1 for *DLH*, Wk-Nr 0002 was delivered to the Luftwaffe upon the outbreak of war as a C-1, prototype V11. After testing at Rechlin it was assigned to 1./KG 40 in April 1940. Note the wingless and tailless Condor fuselage on blocks just in front of the hangar

aircraft seen going south five miles east of Harstad. "Red 1" approached with back to sun and enemy aircraft engaged ten miles southeast of Harstad. Return tracer from single upper turret gun silenced after first burst. After several more bursts white smoke came from engines and trail of white smoke from port wing root. Enemy aircraft speed 250-300 mph, dirty green camouflage with black cross on white ground either side of fuselage. Return fire was observed again just before ammunition ran out. Enemy aircraft was going down towards sea when combat finished.'

I./KG 40 lost a second Condor to RAF fighters on 29 May, the aeroplane being shot down by Plt Off Neville Banks of No 46 Sqn, resulting in the deaths of Leutnant Otto Freytag and his crew – Banks was killed later that same day. Another Fw 200 had been damaged in an accident at Oslo-Gardermoen 24 hours earlier. Despite these losses, it was clear that the Condor had proved its worth.

In order to achieve the 2400 km combat radius that the Luftwaffe desired, Focke-Wulf Flugzeugbau's Technical Director, Kurt Tank, had six 300-litre fuel tanks installed un what had previously been the Condor's passenger compartment. Totally unprotected, these tanks were highly vulnerable to tracer or incendiary rounds

Able to range over long distances, the aeroplane was credited with sinking a number of ships on 25 and 29 April 1940. The most spectacular success, however, came on 10 June, when Oberleutnant Heinrich Schlosser (formerly a Dornier Do 17 reconnaissance pilot with 1 (*Fern*)/*Auklärungsgruppe* 120 (1(F)/120) who had flown in the Polish campaign) sank the 13,242 British Registered Tonnage (BRT) HMS *Vandyck* off Narvik. This ex-liner had been converted into an armed troop transport upon the outbreak of war, and its sinking resulted in two officers and five ratings being killed and 29 officers and 132 ratings being taken prisoner.

Eight Condors had also been used as transports during the Norwegian campaign by 4./KGzbV 107 and 2./KGzbV 108, the former unit having lost one aircraft in an accident on 22 April 1940. However, numbers available for the transport role were very limited, the priority for the Condor being I./KG 40. As such, their effectiveness as troop transporters was negligible.

With production still to ramp up by the spring of 1940, the Condor was a rare aircraft in the frontline. Those in service were struggling with poor serviceability, and this would continue to be the Fw 200's main Achilles' heel throughout World War 2.

The Condor's most spectacular success during the Norwegian campaign came on 10 June 1940 when Oberleutnant Heinrich Schlosser sank the 13,242 BRT HMS *Vandyck* off Narvik

BATTLE OF BRITAIN

With the Norwegian campaign over, I./KG 40 returned to its home airfield at Lüneburg, in northern Germany, where the arrival of additional Condors allowed the formation of 2./KG 40, to be commanded by 33-year-old Hauptmann Fritz Fliegel. An *Ausbildungsstaffel*/KG 40, equipped with Heinkel He 111s, also existed during the summer of 1940 to train new crews, but it was apparently adsorbed into KG 28 in December 1940 when 3./KG 40 was formed. A bespoke Fw 200 *Erganzungsstaffel* was established in April 1941. Petersen could now start calling himself a *Gruppenkommandeur*, and command of 1. *Staffel* went to 34-year-old Austrian pilot Hauptmann Roman Steszyn.

During July 1940 I./KG 40 was also operating from Marx, near Wilhemshaven, and as part of 9 *Fliegerdivision* (subordinate to *Luftflotte* 2) it was soon undertaking mining and reconnaissance missions around Britain. The Luftwaffe felt confident enough to use the Condors of

An early casualty, this Fw 200C-1 suffered an accident at Oslo-Gardermoen airport on 28 May 1940 during the Norwegian campaign. The aircraft has a pair of Panzer IIs assigned to move it away from the runway

This Fw 200 V2 also came to grief at Oslo-Gardermoen in late May 1940. The aeroplane is Wk-Nr 2884 GC+GC, formerly D-AETA *Westfalen*. Note that the aircraft appears to have a ventral gondola. The Condor is thought to have been flying with 4./KGzbv 107 (and possibly 10./KGrzbv 172 before that) at the time of its accident

Hauptmann Fritz Fliegel was given command of 2./KG 40 upon its formation at Lüneburg during the early summer of 1940. A veteran bomber pilot prior to switching to the Condor, he would eventually take over I./KG 40 from Major Edgar Petersen and receive the *Ritterkreuz* for his numerous combat successes. Fliegel would be killed in action attacking convoy OB 346 on 18 July 1941

I./KG 40 on these somewhat hazardous missions, in addition to the unit's more usual armed reconnaissance flights off the German and French coasts. However, although there were no credible RAF nightfighter defences, the Condor's vulnerability quickly became apparent. On the night of 20 July 1940 a Condor flown by the *Staffelkapitän* of 1./KG 40, Hauptmann Roman Steszyn, was shot down by AA fire when it strayed too close to Hartlepool during a mining sortie to the Firth of Forth. Steszyn, whose body was washed ashore in Holland, and three others were killed, while two were captured. Four nights later the Condor flown by Hauptmann Volkmar Zenker of 2./KG 40 was also lost on a similar mission to Belfast harbour, as he subsequently recalled;

'We took off from Lüneburg and then refuelled at Brest, and there we were loaded with two tons of magnetic mines. Our orders were to drop these in the shipping lanes of Belfast harbour. We only managed to drop three mines before disaster struck.

'I had descended from 1800 metres over the Irish Sea. The engines were idling as I was hoping not to be detected. During the first part of the mission I was flying at 100 metres, but then I opened the throttles very slowly, hoping to go lower and to get rid of the last mine, which had become stuck in its holder. I succeeded, but by now we were at an altitude of 15 metres. When I opened the throttles further the two port engines stopped and the plane banked suddenly. In order to avoid the wingtip hitting the water, I stopped the starboard engines and ditched. The plane had not run out of fuel, by the way, but there had been an air blockage in the fuel lines caused by the long glide with idling engines.

'After ditching, the plane sank pretty fast. The radio operator and a gunner were able to leave by the main door and get out the dinghy. The co-pilot, flight engineer and myself were trapped in the cockpit because the hatch had stuck. I tried to send them aft but we were already under water. I dived through the aircraft and reached the surface of the water inside the fuselage close to the door. I waited for the two others for a moment, then joined the two who were swimming with the inflated dinghy. We expected the missing crew members, who were uninjured and able to swim, but they apparently panicked trying to leave by the safety hatch on top of the cockpit roof or the windows, which were too narrow to let them escape. Because we did not know how soon the plane would sink, we did not dare try a rescue underwater. After a few moments the aircraft sank.

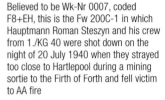

Believed to be Wk-Nr 0007, coded F8+EH, this is the Fw 200C-1 in which Hauptmann Roman Steszyn and his crew from I./KG 40 were shot down on the night of 20 July 1940 when they strayed too close to Hartlepool during a mining sortie to the Firth of Forth and fell victim to AA fire

'The dinghy proved to be our next problem – the self-inflating mechanism didn't work as the CO_2 bottle was empty, so we had to pump it up with bellows. This kept us busy for nearly 45 minutes. One oar was lost during the hubbub and we couldn't reach the coast while it was still dark, though we tried hard, knowing that we were not too far from the border of Southern Ireland.'

The following morning the three survivors were picked up 15 miles northeast of Belfast, by which time they had worked on a story to mislead the British, as a Royal Navy report on their capture reveals;

'On the morning of 24 July three German airmen were rescued from a rubber float by the antisubmarine warfare (ASW) trawler HMS *Paynter* close to Blackhead and landed at Larne. When interrogated, they stated their machine, an He 111, had crashed in the early hours of the morning during a reconnaissance flight over the area, with the loss of two lives.'

Both Fw 200Cs seen here are marked with I./KG 40's 'World in a Ring' unit badge. The aeroplane in the foreground is being refuelled, the Condor having no fewer than six unarmoured fuel tanks within its fuselage

With the loss of Hauptmanns Steszyn and Zenker the Condor had proved to be unsuitable as a minelayer. Furthermore, the destruction of two aeroplanes on such missions in the space of four days, when Focke-Wulf was able to produce only an average of three aircraft a month, made it obvious that the future for I./KG 40 was limited unless changes were made. As a result Petersen then took matters into his own hands;

'In desperation I telephoned Generalmajor [Hans] Jeschonnek [the Luftwaffe's Chief of the General Staff] in person. We had served together in the secret air force in Russia in 1929, so we knew each other quite well. I told him the position, and said, "This wasteful business of mining will have to stop, otherwise we will lose all our planes and crews." Jeschonnek was taken aback by my outburst, but said he would look into the matter. My call had the desired effect, because a few days later we received orders to discontinue minelaying.'

By his own admission, Zenker confirmed during his interrogation that Condors were now flying from French bases, thus enabling the Luftwaffe to operate over the western United Kingdom and Atlantic almost with impunity. From June 1940 I./KG 40 had also been able to fly missions from Le Culot and Brussels, in Belgium, and two months later the first Condors arrived at Bordeaux-Mérignac, in southwestern France. From here they were able to fly far out into the Atlantic – something they would do for almost the next four years. However, despite the aircraft's potential, Condor numbers remained limited. For example, on 13 August 1940, out of a strength of nine aircraft, only four were serviceable. Three weeks later I./KG 40 had only seven aircraft on strength, of which just four were serviceable.

Despite its paucity in numbers, the Condor registered its first success of the Battle of Britain on 13 August when an unidentified 8000-ton freighter was damaged northeast of the Irish coast. The first named ship to be attacked was the Norwegian freighter *Svein Jarl* five days later. Damaged and trailing oil, it limped back to Londonderry for repairs (*Svein Jarl* was eventually sunk by U-95 on 24 February 1941).

A close-up of the famous 'World in a Ring' unit badge that adorned KG 40's Fw 200s and was inspired by the *Geschwader*'s long-range maritime mission

The first confirmed success by a Condor operating from Brest occurred on 25 August 1940. Now part of IV. *Fliegerkorps* (subordinate to *Luftflotte* 3), a Condor took off from Brest at 0707 hrs to search for a convoy. The crew failed to find its target convoy, but at 1430 hrs it spotted the 3821 BRT *Goathland* 630 km west of Land's End. The *Goathland* was sailing from Pepel, in Sierra Leone, to Belfast with a cargo of iron ore. The Condor made three bombing runs over the freighter, the first two resulting in two near misses by 250 kg bombs, but on the third attack the bomb hit the No 2 cargo hold and the freighter began to sink at 1500 hrs at 50° 21N, 14° 50W. Despite being machine-gunned on each run, the 36 crew members climbed into two lifeboats without any casualties, and all survived. One lifeboat with 18 survivors was picked up by the Irish ship *Lanarhone*.

A point of particular interest is that the *Goathland*'s captain described the Condor as having a badge he described as 'A white ball having a wide yellow ring around it resembling the planet Saturn'. The attack must have been made at

The 5702-tonne SS *Starstone* was attacked west of Donegal by Feldwebel Bernhard Flinsch of 2./KG 40 on 31 October 1940. Like many merchantmen at this time, the vessel was lightly armed. Despite being badly damaged, SS *Starstone* survived the attack and returned to service in 1941

particularly low level – the standard tactic at this time – to have enabled the ship's crew to see the newly painted I./KG 40 'World in a Ring' badge on the nose.

Despite the unit's limited numbers, it was now clear that with I./KG 40 firmly established in France, far from the attention of RAF fighters, it could fly armed reconnaissance missions as far as 24° west with little fear of being shot down, preying on undefended merchant ships, and at the same time keeping the Kriegsmarine, and in particular *Marine Gruppe West*, happy by acting as its eyes and ears. A good example of this occurred on 17 September 1940 when a Condor crew that had taken off just after midnight reported at 0730 hrs that it had spotted an unescorted convoy comprising five large and ten medium freighters in location 15° West/7612, headed 300°. Then, at 0745 hrs, the crew reported another convoy of nine large and two small freighters, with an escort of three destroyers, in location 15° West/7635, headed 130°.

Some 45 minutes later the crew spotted and identified the 5152-ton SS *Kalliopi S*, which had broken away from the convoy northwest of the Irish island of Inishtrahull the previous day and was headed for Limerick. The Condor attacked the defenceless ship 11 miles off Tory, hitting it with a single bomb that set it on fire. The crew took to lifeboats and the freighter later drifted ashore at Sheepshaven Bay, still on fire.

This was now proving to be a golden time for the Condor, one pilot writing post-war, 'The convoys, even quite large ones, often sailed with hardly any air defences at all. On the Condor we could carry only a few bombs, but we could go in very low when attacking and make every one count.' Unarmed merchantmen could do nothing to defend themselves, which allowed Condors to make low-level and thus accurate attacks at mast height. There was no real need for a bombsight. The bomb

Proudly wearing the *Ritterkreuz* around his neck, Oberleutnant Bernhard Jope of I./KG 40 received this decoration after crippling the 42,500 GRT troopship *Empress of Britain* on 26 October 1940.

release mechanism was set to give eight-metre spacing between bombs. As Edgar Petersen said after the war, 'You could hardly miss, even without a bombsight. At least one of the bombs would find the ship as long as you kept low enough.'

By 31 December 1940 the *Gruppe* had been credited with sinking some 800,000 Gross Registered Tonnage (GRT) of shipping for the loss of just two Condors, both written off in accidents on operational sorties. The first occurred on 20 August 1940, when Oberleutnant Kurt-Heinrich Mollenhauser's Fw 200C-1 of 1./*KG* 40 became lost owing to a navigation error in bad weather and hit Faha Mountain near Cloghane, in County Kerry. The second, an Fw 200C-2 flown by Oberleutnant Theodor Schuldt, *Staffelführer* of 2./KG 40, went missing to the west of Ireland, Schuldt's body and that of one other crewman later being washed ashore.

Condors were still rare beasts (by the start of January 1941 I./KG 40 still had only 12 aircraft on strength), and combats between Fw 200s and RAF Coastal Command aircraft were extremely infrequent. The first recorded engagement took place on 14 August 1940 when a Short Sunderland of No 210 Sqn was encountered 130 miles off Bloody Foreland, the flying boat being damaged in the clash. Just over a month later, on 25 September, the crew of a Sunderland from No 10 Sqn RAAF reported an inconclusive combat off the Irish coast at 0811 hrs. On 11 October another inconclusive combat took place with an Avro Anson of No 48 Sqn (the aircraft was reported by the Germans as a 'Bristol Blenheim'). On 24 October a Lockheed Hudson of No 269 Sqn claimed to have damaged a Condor off Ireland and, finally, on 3 December it was the turn of a Saunders-Roe Lerwick of No 209 Sqn to have an inconclusive combat with an Fw 200 260 miles northwest of Ireland. The KG 40 crew recognised their assailant as being a Lerwick. In all cases the personnel involved recorded the details of the combat and returned to base undamaged.

Oberleutnant Jope reports to Major Petersen immediately after returning to Bordeaux-Mérignac following his successful attack on the *Empress of Great Britain*

The most successful Condor mission of the war to date occurred on 26 October 1940 when Oberleutnant Bernhard Jope of 2./KG 40 crippled the 42,500 GRT troopship *Empress of Britain*. Later to become one of the best-known Fw 200 pilots, and awarded the *Ritterkreuz mit Eichenlaub* (Knight's Cross with Oakleaves), Jope joined I./KG 40 in the summer of 1940 as a pilot with 2. *Staffel*. Acting as the *Gruppe* Technical Officer (a position later to be filled by Oberleutnant Ernst Hetzel) because of his university background, Jope was awarded the Iron Cross First Class in September 1940. At the end of the following month he carried out a mission that brought him immediately to the attention of not only the German public but also the British military.

After taking off from Bordeaux-Mérignac on an armed reconnaissance over the Atlantic at 0409 hrs on 26 October, Jope located a 42,500 GRT liner 140 km west of the Isle of Aran at 1030 hrs. This was the *Empress of Britain*, which was being used as a troop transporter. It was Britain's second largest vessel, and the tenth largest merchant ship in the world. Jope attacked without hesitation, dropping six 250 kg bombs, two of which hit the target. The liner was crippled and caught fire, and the German crew heard the SOS message being transmitted. Jope's Condor was in turn lightly damaged by AA fire. Having reported what he had achieved, he turned for home. The liner, in fact, had been mortally hit, with at least 25 merchant seamen killed. Although the vessel was taken into tow, it was to no avail. The vessel's location had been transmitted to U-32, commanded by Oberleutnant-zur-See Hans Jenisch, and the U-boat sank it two days later (U-32 was in turn sunk on 30 October 1940, with Jenisch being made a PoW).

The bombing of the *Empress of Britain* was a propaganda coup for the Luftwaffe, and Jope's achievement was widely reported. On 30 December 1940 he received the *Ritterkreuz*. As a point of interest, Jenisch had already been presented with the same award on 7 October 1940, having sunk 16 ships and damaged three more.

As the maritime war was starting to escalate, the air war over Great Britain continued. Contrary to popular belief, Condors did not attack mainland Britain in daylight in great numbers, but there is evidence of a limited number of dusk, dawn or nighttime attacks. On 14 October 1940, for example, Oberleutnant Hans Buchholz of 1./KG 40 took off at 0130 hrs with his Condor laden with five 250 kg bombs to attack the Rolls-Royce factory at Hillingdon, near Glasgow, which he duly did at 0716 hrs. Seven days later he tried to repeat the attack, but had to abandon the mission owing to heavy cloud cover.

At breakfast time on 29 November 1940 three unidentified crews attempted to attack Glasgow. One reported dropping two 500 kg bombs, 12 50 kg bombs and 60 incendiaries on the northwest suburbs. A second crew attacked Falkirk with a similar bomb load because of poor weather over Glasgow, while the final crew, also due to the weather, dropped a similar bomb load south of Glasgow. On 30 November Oberleutnant Hans-Joachim Hase of 2./KG 40 reported attacking Glasgow, but it is believed that he was one of the crews involved in the previous day's operations. It was thought that a Condor attacked an aluminium plant and power station at Fort William on 22 December 1940, but this is now

Shortly after dawn on 14 October 1940 Oberleutnant Hans Buchholz of 1./KG 40 dropped five 250 kg bombs on the Rolls-Royce factory at Hillingdon, near Glasgow. Seven days later he tried to repeat the attack, but had to abandon the mission owing to heavy cloud cover over the target

Oberleutnant Hans-Joachim Hase (right) flew one of three Fw 200s from 2./KG 40 that attempted to attack Glasgow during the morning of 29 November 1940. Only one aircraft managed to drop their ordnance on target due to poor weather over the Scottish city

Meteorologist Dr Friedo Ehrhardt completed 41 operational flights with I./KG 40. He made the first of these on 2 October 1940, and had Oberleutnant Hase as his pilot for the missions on 17 and 25 December that same year

believed to have been a Ju 88 of 1(*F*)/120 commanded by Oberleutnant Siegfried Fidorra. However, Condors almost certainly attacked shipping at Loch Sunari, southwest of Fort William, on this date, and the following day they targeted vessels in the Firth of Lorne near Oban. Finally, an embarrassing attack is thought to have occurred on the night of 20-21 December when an inexperienced I./KG 40 crew became confused during an attack on Liverpool and bombed Dublin intead.

As the Battle of Britain came to a close, the anti-shipping war now truly began to escalate. A good indication of the heightened intensity is well illustrated by the logbook of meteorologist Dr Friedo Ehrhardt, who completed 41 operational flights with I./KG 40. He made the first of these on 2 October 1940, with Oberleutnant Heinrich Schlosser as his pilot, and took part in the sinking of the 2218 GRT SS *Latymer*. Six of the ship's crew were killed and 22 rescued. Having undertaken eight sorties in October, Ehrhardt then flew with Oberleunant Bernhard Jope on 3 and 24 November (attacking the SS *Windsor Castle* during the first sortie). He was part of Oberleutnant Hans Buchholz's crew on 6 and 13 November (damaging three freighters during the first sortie and attacking SS *Empire Wind* on the second), and then flew with Oberleunant Friedrich Burmeister on 9 and 17 November and 28 December (attacking the SS *Empress of Japan* on the 9 November mission). Ehrhardt switched to Hauptmann Roman Dawcyznski's crew on 21 November, flew with Oberleunant Hans-Joachim Hase on 17 and 25 December, and, finally, completed a mission with an unidentified NCO pilot on 22 December.

Still with no credible threat from Allied aircraft, the Condor crews continued to attack the predominantly undefended ships from very low level, normally dropping just four 250 kg bombs, which would hit either just above or just below the waterline. As a result the Condor and its crews rapidly began to make a name for themselves, and by early 1941 I./KG 40 already had five *Ritterkreuz* winners, although two of these men would be dead by July 1941 – proof that ships' anti-Condor defences were at long last starting to improve. More Condor pilots were to be awarded

The tail of a I./KG 40 Condor, showing both the number of missions flown by the aeroplane (28, according to the tally beneath the swastika) and successes from 28 August through to 15 November 1940. The lack of Fw 200s in the frontline in 1940-41 meant that crews routinely shared aircraft. Therefore, missions and anti-shipping successes were applied to the tails of the aircraft they were flying at the time – this particular haul was almost certainly the work of several crews

this coveted medal as the maritime war intensified and as Germany's good fortune, despite the setback of the Battle of Britain, continued. It seemed that 1941 would be a good year for the Luftwaffe's maritime air war.

Changes now occurred in the leadership. In November 1940 Major Edgar Petersen was replaced by Hauptmann Fritz Fliegel, who had been temporarily transferred to Berlin in October 1940, while Fliegel's place as *Staffelkapitän* of 2./KG 40 had already been filled by Hauptmann Roman Dawczynski. In December 1940 3./KG 40 became operational, commanded by Oberleutnant Rudolf Mons.

CHAPTER TWO

1941 – BATTLE OF THE ATLANTIC BEGINS

1./KG 40's F8+CH, parked between wooden anti-blast walls at Bordeaux-Mérignac in the spring of 1941, displays two shipping successes on its tail. It is believed that this aeroplane is Fw 200C-3 Wk-Nr 0026, in which Hauptmann Konrad Verlohr was reported missing on 24 July 1941

There was a lull in shipping attacks between 19 December 1940 and the sinking of the 6663 GRT *Clytoneus* by Oberleutnant Rudolf Mons on 8 January 1941. Mons took off at 0500 hrs on a weather/armed reconnaissance mission west of Ireland. Just over six hours later, when he and his crew were 480 km northwest of Donegal Bay, they dropped six 250 kg bombs, hitting the vessel (which was en route to Ellesmere Port with a cargo of sugar from Macassar, in southern Africa) with at least two of them and leaving it dead in the water and listing to starboard.

A notable success occurred eight days later when Hauptmann Konrad Verlohr (1./KG 40) and Oberleutnant Bernhard Jope (2./KG 40) attacked convoy OB 274, comprising 40 ships and a strong escort. They were credited with sinking the 6256 GRT *Onoba* and 4581 GRT *Meandros*. January continued to be a good month for I./KG 40, the unit sinking a total of 17 ships for the loss of just one aircraft in combat – Oberleutnant Friedrich Burmeister's Fw 200C-3 was shot down by light AA fire while attacking HMS *Seaman* on 10 January. Burmeister and two of his crew were rescued and three were killed, the oberleutnant's capture offering the Allies a chance to find out more about I./KG 40.

On 28 January I./KG 40 carried out a major attack with five aircraft, probably against convoy HX 102. Between 1110 hrs and 1225 hrs attacks were made by four crews. Oberleutnant Heinrich Schlosser, formerly of 2./KG 40 but now flying with the recently formed 3./KG 40, reported hitting a 4600-ton freighter 560 km west-northwest of Tory Island with four 250 kg bombs. Oberleutnant Hans Buchholz of 1./KG 40 carried out a similar attack on a 6000/8000-ton freighter 450 km west of Castle Bay with unknown results. Next, Hauptmann Edmund Daser of 1./KG 40 reported attacking a convoy 290 km west of Colonsay with one 500 kg and two 250 kg bombs, hitting a 4500-ton freighter with unrecorded results. Finally, Hauptmann Fritz Fliegel attacked a convoy 260 km west of Tobermory, noting that one bomb detonated under a ship. Oberleutnant Hans-Jochen Bobsien of 2./KG 40 failed to find any targets.

The Allies recorded two attacks by Condors on 28 January, with the SS *Grelrosa* being hit 400 miles west of Northern Ireland. It was heading to the Tyne from New York with a cargo of wheat, the ship sinking with the loss of five crew – 31 seamen were saved, however. The SS *Pandion* was hit 150 miles west of Malin Head, the vessel eventually foundering in Lough Swilly on 30 January.

If January 1941 had been good for I/KG 40, February was even better, as illustrated by the events of just three days that month. On the 9th five Condors took off from Bordeaux-Mérignac to attack convoy HG 53, sailing southwest of Portugal. The five aircraft commanders were all highly experienced – Hauptmann Fritz Fliegel and Oberleutnants Heinrich Schlosser, Bernhard Jope, Hans Buchholz and Erich Adam. The first four officers duly became recipients of the *Ritterkreuz*, with Jope having already received the award.

Erich Adam's Condor was damaged by the sloop HMS *Deptford*, forcing him to break off his attack and force-land at Moura, in Portugal, but the remaining four crews all enjoyed success. Schlosser was credited with sinking three ships totalling 8500 tonnes, Fliegel claimed two ships totalling 11,000 tonnes and damaged a third, Jope was credited with sinking one of 5000 tonnes and damaging another and Buchholz damaged

Oberleutnant Rudolf Mons and his crew claimed I./KG 40's first success of 1941 when they sank the 6663 GRT *Clytoneus* on 8 January 480 km northwest of Donegal Bay

Hauptmann Fritz Fliegel (with ruler) is seen here deep in conversation with Hauptmann Edmund Daser at Bordeaux-Mérignac. Both men were involved in a major attack on 30-ship-strong convoy HX 102 by five aircraft from I./KG 40 on 28 January 1941. The vessels had departed Halifax on 11 January bound for Liverpool. Daser claimed to have hit a 4500-ton freighter 290 km west of Colonsay, whilst Fliegel attacked a convoy 260 km west of Tobermory, noting that one bomb detonated under a ship

Fw 200C-3s of I./KG 40 are prepared for their next long-range missions at a damp Bordeaux-Mérignac in early 1941. The nearest aircraft, coded F8+DL, boasts mission markings and a single ship silhouette on its fin that denote successes for its crews

Officers from I./KG 40 are briefed by meteorologist Dr Soltau at Bordeaux-Mérignac prior to heading out on offensive patrols over the Atlantic. They are, in the foreground, from left to right, Leutnants Robert Maly and Ernst Burkard, Dr Soltau, Dr Freido Ehrhardt (with glasses, in the background), Hauptmann Fritz Fliegel, unknown, unknown (in the background), Oberleutnants Bernhard Jope and Heinrich Schlosser, Dr Schlosser(?) and Oberleutnant Rudolph Mons (far right)

one. Confirmed losses were the *Varna*, *Jura*, *Britannic*, *Dagmar I* and *Tejo*. At the same time as the Condors were wreaking death and destruction, Leutnant zur See Nicolai von Clausen in U-37 sank the *Courland* and *Estrellano*. It was a remarkable achievement for the Germans, and in particular for I./KG 40. Fliegel's success almost certainly hastened his receipt of the *Ritterkreuz* on 25 March 1941, Buchholz having been presented with the same award the previous day.

The 19th was the second significant date in February, with Bernhard Jope again being in the thick of the action. During an armed weather reconnaissance off the Hebrides he came across convoy OB 287. What happened next is detailed in his post-mission report;

'Approach flight west of Ireland, strong headwinds, which calmed down west of the Hebrides, showers of rain. After flying through the clouds for a while the convoy suddenly appeared in PlQ 16 West 7004°, course west, 45 merchant ships up to 10,000 tons, few escorts. Immediately flew a surprise attack on the left line of three ships ahead. Three bombs were dropped on the first ship (8000 tons), two behind the stern and the third hit the quarterdeck. The second ship was left out and, approaching from behind, the third one was attacked with three bombs. One bomb was a direct hit into the engine house with a corresponding explosion of the boiler. Because of lack of fuel it was not possible to transmit radio beams for the U-boats. The attack took place at 1330 hrs. Because of the surprise of the attack no defensive actions could be observed. Two barrage balloons were seen about 50 metres above two of the ships.

'Before the convoy was sighted a few patrol boats and a tugboat towing a loaded merchant ship, course east, were observed west and southwest of the Hebrides, but were not attacked. An aircraft was also seen near the merchant ship.

Oberleutnant Erich Adam (left) and his crew are welcomed back to Bordeaux-Mérignac upon their return from Portugal. He had had to force-land his Condor at Moura on 9 February 1941 after it had been damaged by AA fire from the sloop HMS *Deptford* during an attack on convoy HG 53. Standing next to Adam are Feldwebel Paul Hecht (second pilot) and Unteroffizier Kurt Dreyer (radio operator)

'The flight was continued at an altitude of 600-800 m, with two-tenths of cloud, via Fair Island between the Orkneys and the Shetlands to Stavanger.'

Jope's claims were correct, as the Allies reported the loss of the 5642 GRT tanker *Gracia* and the 5539 GRT freighter *Housatonic*. To add to his success, on the way back from Stavanger two days later Jope came across the same convoy, and he filed the following report;

'Approach flight from Stavanger, via Fair Island, to the calculated position of the convoy that had already been attacked on 19 and 20 February. It was still dark when the lights of a ship were sighted about 250 km northwest of the Hebrides at about 0800 hrs. The ship's lights were turned off immediately but several attacks were carried out in the moonlight, an SC 250 bomb was dropped and the ship was also gunned with cannon and machine gun fire. But there was no visible effect.

'At 1030 hrs the convoy was sighted and, using the moment of surprise, was attacked as well. Two of the tankers, sailing at the back of the convoy, were bombed with three bombs each. The 5000-ton tanker was damaged

Hardworking groundcrew wheel a SC 250 general purpose bomb towards a Condor of I./KG 40 at Bordeaux-Mérignac in the summer of 1941. Fw 200s could carry up to four of these 250 kg weapons. Inspired by its emblem, the unit adorned the noses of a number of its early Fw 200s with the names of planets or constellations – this aeroplane was *Mars*.

by a bomb detonation next to the hull at the stern. A direct hit destroyed the 3000-ton tanker – the bomb went off in the engine house, destroyed the superstructure on the quarterdeck and subsequently the boiler exploded [both of the ships fell back behind the convoy and were supported by two auxiliary vessels].

'After the attack all ships opened fire. We were flying in circles around the convoy for about 20 minutes. After the message "staying at the convoy and sending radio signals/radio beacon on the U-boat frequency", radio signals/radio beacon for the U-boats were transmitted.

The return of Oberleutnant Bernhard Jope (saluting, facing the camera) to Bordeaux-Mérignac from Stavanger on 21 February 1941. He had attacked convoy OR 287 during the flight, sinking the tanker *Scottish Standard* (6999 tonnes) and damaging two more vessels. He had sunk two ships from the same convoy 48 hours earlier

'During the return flight at an altitude of 3500 m there was a strong back-wind. After reaching the southwest corner of Ireland it was possible to calculate the exact position of the convoy by dead reckoning.'

As confirmation of this attack, on 22 February 1941 the Germans reported;

'Yesterday, bomber aircraft attacked British merchant ships off the east and west coasts of England. A 4000-ton steamship was sunk, and two big tankers as well as several other ships were seriously damaged.'

Later the same day I./KG 40 received the following signal;

'On 21 February 1941, 1030 hrs (or 1130 hrs), the position of the obviously damaged British tanker *Scottish Standard* (6999 tons gross) was 5918° N/1612° W (180 nautical miles west of Rosemary Bank, PlQ AL 3494). To support the ship, tugs and escorts (possibly destroyers, too) were sent out at 0230 hrs on 22 February.'

The full success of the action was confirmed by a similar signal the next day;

Still wearing his flying overalls, Oberleutnant Jope provides a verbal report of the convoy attack to his *Gruppenkommandeur*, Hauptmann Fritz Fliegel, on 21 February 1941. To Jope's left, wearing the forage cap, is Oberleutnant Heinrich Schlosser

'OKM B. command reports on 23 February 1941. As a result of the airborne attack on the outgoing convoy Onset two steamships had been damaged and are now waiting for tug support. During the evening of 22 February the tugs *Thames*, *St Olaves*[?] and *Northern Spray* were informed that the tanker *Scottish Standard* (6999 tons gross) had gone down. The vessels were then sent – with top priority – to support the steamship *Kingston Hill* [not registered]. At 1535 hrs the position was 5958° N, 1222° W.'

February 1941 proved to mark the zenith of I./KG 40's successes, with five more ships sunk on the 26th (credited to Leutnant Otto Gose and Oberleutnants Heinrich Schlosser and Rudolf Mons) and another three the following day. Condors, together with U-boats – in particular U-47, commanded by Kapitänleutnant Günther Prien – had a field day with convoy OB 290, sinking 13 ships and damaging a further five.

There were just two Condor combat losses during the month. In addition to Erich Adam's landing in Portugal, on 5 February Oberleutnant Paul Gömmer and his crew from 1./KG 40 were killed while trying to force-land their Fw 200C-3 in southern Ireland after it was damaged by AA fire.

Although more successes would come the Fw 200's way well into 1941, the Allies were now taking action to combat what would later be called the 'Condor Menace'. Improved AA guns and more escorts for convoys soon forced Fw 200 crews to fly higher, and when more Allied aircraft – particularly carrier-borne fighters – appeared within convoys, Condor pilots had to adopt a more cautious approach to their attacks. Yet despite the eventual presence of Fighter Catapult Ships (FCS) and Catapult Aircraft Merchant (CAM) vessels, armed with Hurricane Is, and, eventually, Martlet fighters onboard escort carriers, most Condor losses were attributable to AA fire or accidents. Operational Fw 200 losses for the first half of 1941 amounted to five aircraft downed by AA fire, one destroyed by an enemy aircraft and three lost to unknown causes.

The first reported air-to-air combat occurred northwest of Rockall on 11 January 1941 when a Sunderland of No 201 Sqn engaged a Condor. The flying boat crew claimed to have damaged the Fw 200. On 29 January an Fw 200C-3 flown by Oberleutnant Erich Adam of 2./KG 40 clashed with a Sunderland flown by Flg Off Barry Aikman of No 210 Sqn. The flying boat's rear gunner, Sgt Reg Williamson, was wounded and the Condor's radio operator, Leutnant Alfred Winter, killed when he was shot in the head.

The German combat report following the action makes interesting reading. Having taken off at 0602 hrs on an armed reconnaissance, the Fw 200 crew engaged the Sunderland at 1237 hrs (1137 hrs British Summer Time) in grid 25° West/3640. A running battle ensued, the Sunderland crew using machine guns and their counterparts in the Condor also firing machine guns and 20 mm cannon. The Condor was hit 15 times, suffering damage to the starboard outer engine and navigational equipment. Its gunners in turn reported hitting the Sunderland, which was last seen flying away trailing dark smoke behind it. Almost three months would pass before a Coastal Command aircraft finally achieved its first confirmed Condor kill.

At the start of March 1941 more changes began to occur that would affect I./KG 40. Subordinate to *Luftflotte* 3, *Fliegerführer Atlantik* was created, based at Brandérion, a small village east of Lorient in Brittany. The unit, commanded by Oberstleutnant Martin Harlinghausen, would carry out armed reconnaissance on behalf of *Befehlshaber der U-Boote* – I./KG 40 had been placed under the latter's command in January of that year. Reporting the positions and movements of Allied shipping to assist U-boat attacks, *Fliegerführer Atlantik*'s secondary task (not normally carried out by Condors) was conventional attacks on shipping in British coastal waters. Fw 200s would only attack shipping further out to sea that was well out of range of land-based day and nightfighters.

Oberstleutnant Martin Harlinghausen was made commander of the newly created *Fliegerführer Atlantik* in early March 1941, his unit being responsible for performing armed reconnaissance (with a variety of aircraft, including the Condors of I./KG 40) on behalf of *Befehlshaber der U-Boote*

By March 1941 I./KG 40 had 21 Condors on strength, but serviceability remained poor – at one stage during the month it had only six airworthy aircraft. Nevertheless, the *Gruppe* had by now expanded in size to four *Staffeln* (three operational and one training), while a further two *Gruppen* were also formed, albeit not equipped with the Fw 200. In January 1941 4./KG 40, commanded by Hauptmann Paul Fischer, was formed, flying the He 111, and a further two *Staffeln* were established in May, flying the Do 217 (4./KG 40 also converted to the Dornier bomber from June onwards). Initially, 4./KG 40 came under the control of I./KG 40, but when expanded to *Gruppe* strength it was commanded by Hauptmann Wendt Freiherr von Schlippenbach. In March 1941 III./KG 40, commanded by Major Walter Herbold, was also formed from I./KG 1 – the unit flew He 111H-3s. In July 1941 Herbold was replaced by anti-shipping expert Hauptmann Robert Kowalewski, formerly of II./KG 26 and a good friend of Oberstleutnant Harlinghausen.

Despite having suffered relatively few losses, I./KG 40 was still having problems performing its assigned tasks. This situation worsened when Major Edgar Petersen returned as *Geschwaderkommodore* of KG 40 in April 1941, for he wanted to carry out massed or wave attacks with his Condors due to the success such missions had previously enjoyed. By then there were 25 to 30 Condors on strength, and of these, no more than six to eight were serviceable at any one time. However, newer versions of the Condor were at last coming into service.

The initial Fw 200C-1 had a defensive armament of MG 15 7.92 mm machine guns fore and aft of the dorsal positions and an MG FF 20 mm cannon in the front of the ventral gondola. The aeroplane could also carry up to five 250 kg bombs. Its replacement, the C-2, incorporated attempts to improve on the C-1 in respect of bomb racks, engine nacelles and several internal and structural modifications necessary for a combat aeroplane, as opposed to a civilian transport. The C-3, which slowly became the primary frontline variant during the spring of 1941, embodied engine changes, increased structural weight, increased bomb load, the fitment of a dorsal turret and beam fuselage guns and changes to the calibre and type of several of the guns.

Anti-shipping expert Hauptmann Robert Kowalewski, formerly of II./KG 26, replaced Major Walter Herbold as the *Gruppenkommandeur* of III./KG 40 in July 1941

BLACK PHASE

Between March and July 1941 there was a dramatic rise in the number of Condors lost, both to operational and non-operational causes. In March two Condors were destroyed in accidents, resulting in the deaths of six crewmen, including three pilots. That month (on the 2nd) also saw the first combat between a mainland UK-based Fighter Command unit and a Condor, when two Hurricanes of No 3 Sqn damaged an Fw 200 off Sumburgh, in the Shetland Islands, as recounted in the combat report of Plt Off Doug Robertson;

'When flying over the sea 30 miles east of Sumburgh, I sighted one Fw 200 flying only a few feet over the sea and at the same time heard "Red 1" [Plt Off John Crabb] give the "Tally Ho". I followed "Red 1" into the attack, flying astern and slightly above him. Immediately "Red 1" broke from his first attack, I fired a three-second burst from dead astern and

A series of photographs were taken by Oberleutnant Franz Vuellers' crew during an attack on a convoy on 19 March 1941 in Condor F8+GH. The 5193-tonne merchantman SS *Benvorlich* was sunk during the engagement. As this dramatic shot shows, Vuellers employed low-level attacking passes on the lightly defended vessels in good weather conditions. SS *Benvorlich* was sunk west of Malin Head, in County Donegal, while on passage from Middlesbrough to the Far East. Twenty of its crew were lost

Oberleutnant Vuellers makes a head-on pass at the convoy, this photograph being taken from the rear dorsal gunner's blister turret

This was one of the vessels targeted by Oberleutnant Vuellers and his crew, although it is not the SS *Benvorlich*

observed tracer entering the fuselage of the enemy aircraft. I broke away as "Red 1" was delivering his starboard attack. I climbed to the right and delivered a diving beam attack from 200 ft above, firing a one-second burst. I had to break this attack as "Red 1" was firing from the opposite beam. I then delivered

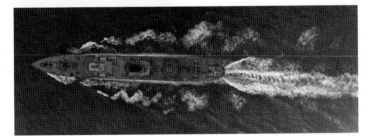

another astern attack, firing a six-second burst from approximately 200 yards range. Again tracer was seen to enter the enemy aircraft. During all these attacks I experienced no return fire.'

Although Robertson reported no return fire, Crabb did, stating it was heavy at first then abruptly stopped. The Fw 200C-3 in question force-landed at Varhaug, south of Stavanger. The only casualty was meteorologist Karl Schwalb, who was injured.

Apparently just three ships were sunk in March, namely the *Benvorlich* on the 19th, the *Beaverbrae* on the 25th and the *Empire Mermaid* the following day. The first and last of these were credited to Oberleutnants Franz Vuellers and Rudolf Mons, respectively (albeit the *Empire Mermaid* did not finally sink until 28 March).

At last, in April, Coastal Command achieved its first confirmed aerial victory over a Condor when, on the 16th, Flt Lt Bill Riley and WO Donaldson, in a Bristol Beaufighter of No 252 Sqn, shot down the Fw 200C-3 flown by Oberleutnant Hermann Richter of 1./KG 40.

Two Condors, two He 111s and a Do 215 were destroyed when 24 Wellingtons from RAF Bomber Command targeted Bordeaux-Mérignac during the night of 12-13 April 1941. Two hangars were also demolished and the airfield infrastructure badly damaged. The tails of the two wrecked Fw 200s can be seen here, sat amongst the charred remains of both aircraft

The aeroplane crashed into the sea off Blacksod Bay, in North County Mayo, its crew of six being reported as missing. Riley's combat report read as follows;

'At the end of the patrol an enemy aircraft was sighted at 1420 hrs on a course of 210 degrees. Identified as a Condor. I started my attack from the beam quarter, finishing up astern. Fire was opened at 300 yards and continued in short bursts to point-blank range when astern. The Condor replied with the midship gun. The Condor caught fire at the rear port wing root, both engines appearing unserviceable. The Condor swung to the left, straightened out, then dived into the sea in flames at an angle of 45 degrees. No survivors and very little wreckage were seen. The Condor was painted entirely green, with crosses silhouetted in white. No lower gondola observed.'

On 17 April Oberleutnant Paul Kalus of 1./KG 40 and his crew were reported missing, and the body of an airman was recovered from the sea on 21 May and buried in the Shetlands. The next day (18 April), Oberleutnant Ernst Müller of 3./KG 40 and his crew ditched off Schull Island, County Cork. They all landed in Ireland, where they were interned. Finally, the Condor flown by Oberleutnant Roland Schelcher of 1./KG 40 was apparently shot down by naval gunfire off the Shetlands on 29 April with the death of the entire crew. Of interest, Schelcher's brother Ekkehard had been killed with *Stab* III./JG 54 on 2 September 1940, his body not being recovered until 1977. In addition, on two successive nights (12-13 and 13-14 April) Bomber Command targeted Bordeaux-Mérignac, destroying an Fw 200C-1, a C-3 and a D-2b that was being used as a photo-reconnaissance aircraft by 3. *Staffel*. The loss of seven Condors in one month, not to mention their crews, was hard for I./KG 40 to absorb as Focke-Wulf was still only producing an average of five aircraft per month.

Again, the number of vessels sunk by Fw 200s was down in April too. On the 6th the SS *Nicolau Zographia*, SS *Olga S* and SS *Dunstan* were sunk, with the successful pilots including Leutnants Rudolf Mayr and Robert Maly of 3. *Staffel*. Ten days later Condors sank the SS *Swedru* and SS *Favorit*, both of which were credited to Oberleutnant Rudolf Heindl of 3./KG 40. Two more ships were sunk towards the end of the month.

There were fewer sinkings (three) and losses (one) in May, although the latter was a bad one for I./KG 40. Just after dawn on the 19th, while a Condor was attacking the SS *Umgeni* off Holywood, Northern Ireland, gunners onboard the ship managed to fire just one round in defence of the vessel, which hit the aircraft's nose and caused it to catch fire. Very shortly afterwards the Fw 200 ditched 500 yards from the ship. Two of its crew had been wounded, and they

Oberleutnant Franz Vuellers was photographed outside I./KG 40's operations building at Bordeaux-Mérignac in 1941

drowned before they could be saved, but the remaining five were rescued uninjured. Amongst those to perish was *Ritterkreuz* holder Oberleutnant Hans Buchholz, his luck having finally run out. Buchholz's death was of great interest to the RAF, as was noted in the intelligence report created following this action;

'The first pilot of this plane was the famous Oberleutnant Hans Buchholz, who has long been praised in the German High Command communiqués and in the German Press for his deeds of valour.

'On 2.3.41, *La Tribunas* reported that at dawn on 29.2.41 he sank a British merchant ship carrying magnesium, some thousands of kilometres west of Ireland. On that date he was credited with the sinking of 24,000 tons and to have seriously damaged a further 15,000 tons. On 14.4.41, the *Völkischer Beobachter* announced that he had been awarded the *Ritterkreuz*. By that date he was credited with the sinking of ten merchant ships totalling 60,800 tons and to have damaged a further eight ships totalling 48,000 tons. Some of these, the report continued, were "so badly damaged that they must be reckoned as lost. Buchholz himself is also unfortunately lost".'

June also saw only one loss in combat when the Fw 200C-3 flown by Oberleutnant Erich Westermann broke up in mid-air on the 15th after suffering damage from AA fire while attacking convoy HG 65. The wreckage crashed on land at Amaeleja in Portugal and all six crew were killed. The Fw 200C-1 flown by Leutnant Otto Gose was also hit by AA fire attacking the same convoy, the crew being forced to land on the short strip (just 1640 ft in length) at Navio, in Spain. The damage inflicted on the Condor had been quite severe, with a fuel tank holed and the flight engineer killed. A Ju 52/3m was subsequently flown in from Bordeaux-Mérignac with spare parts, fuel and groundcrew, the latter

The Finnish tanker *Josefina Thordén* was attacked by Hauptmann Fritz Fliegel and his crew on 19 May 1941. The vessel had been sailing from Galveston, Texas, to the port of Petsamo, in northern Finland, when it was stopped by the ASW trawler HMS *Northern Chief* and ordered to Tórshavn, in the Faroe Islands, for inspection. En route it was attacked by Fliegel's aircraft and set on fire amidships, resulting in the loss of 15 crew. The fire was eventually contained and the ship limped into Tórshavn for repairs

The Buchholz crew, which, after numerous successes, was lost on 19 May 1941 while attacking the SS *Umgeni* off Holywood, Northern Ireland. They are, from left to right, Unteroffizier Meinhard Milde (radio operator, PoW 19 May), Feldwebel Spier (radio operator), Oberleutnant Hans Buchholz (killed 19 May) and Oberfeldwebels Otto Kroke (pilot, PoW 19 May) and Erich Kielke (flight engineer, PoW 19 May)

quickly repairing the aeroplane so that it could return to France on 18 June.

Three Condors were also lost in non-combat related incidents in June. On the 15th an Fw 200A-01 had been destroyed at Aalborg West by an engine fire, and nine days later the crew of a C-3 ditched in the Bay of Biscay. Finally, on the 30th, Oberfeldwebel Herbert Rohrbach's C-3 of 1./KG 40, specially equipped with *Schiffsortungsgerät* air-to-surface-vessel (ASV) radar, disappeared over the Atlantic.

The last day of June also saw another running combat fought between a Condor and a Sunderland, Leutnant Rudolf Feldt of 3. *Staffel* being the commander of the German aircraft and Flg Off Athol 'Attie' Weare of No 10 Sqn RAAF piloting the Sunderland. Yet again, both aircraft shot at each other, which resulted in flight engineer Oberfeldwebel Werner Sieth being wounded and the Sunderland suffering damage to its oil and fuel tanks. LAC Milton Griffin was subsequently awarded a Distinguished Flying Medal for the actions he took to save the aeroplane in the wake of this engagement, as the citation for the decoration explained;

'For personal bravery, tenacity of purpose and devotion to duty whilst employed as a member of a Sunderland aircraft crew. On 30 June 1941, LAC Griffin was first fitter in Sunderland "E"/10 when the aircraft was attacked by a Focke-Wulf 200 southwest of Ushant. The combat was indecisive. A later report was received that the enemy aircraft was making for Brest in order to land wounded. After the engagement, it was found that the port outer engine of the Sunderland was losing quantities of oil. LAC Griffin crawled out into the wing and found two large holes in the bottom of the oil tank. He returned to the hull, obtained tools, plugs and a two-gallon tin of oil and a small preserved fruit tin. He returned to the wing, plugged up the holes, pierced the top of the tank and managed to keep a continuous supply of oil poured into the tank to counteract the loss through leakage.

'LAC Griffin made four journeys into the wing, each time with a two-gallon tin of oil. In all, he was two hours in the wing nursing the engine in intense heat, right alongside the engine and in a very cramped position. In view of the intensity of the enemy fire, it is considered that LAC Griffin's act contributed materially to the safe return of the aircraft to base.'

Sinkings were hard to come by in June, with only two vessels confirmed as destroyed by Condors, on the 6th and 19th. However, encounters with the RAF were increasing considerably. 3. *Staffel* crews encountered Coastal Command aircraft on at least nine occasions during the month, although the RAF logged only two engagements in return.

July also proved to be costly for I./KG 40, with a number of aircraft suffering accidents that seriously reduced the unit's pool of serviceable Condors. On 17 July there was another combat between Coastal Command

and an Fw 200, but this time, despite radio operator Oberleutnant Hans Jordens being killed, Oberleutnant Rudolf Heindl's gunners succeeded in shooting down an Armstrong Whitworth Whitley of No 502 Sqn. The aircraft was being flown by Wg Cdr Donald Shore, who was about to take command of No 612 Sqn. Although he and another crewman were wounded, Shore managed to ditch, thus allowing his five-strong crew to be rescued by HMS *Westcott*. The combat report filed by No 502 Sqn read as follows;

'At 0810 hrs while on anti-submarine escort an aircraft was sighted on the starboard bow flying across the head of convoy OB 346 on a northerly then westerly course at a height of approximately 50 ft. The aircraft was not identified but was taken to be a Hudson on patrol. A shallow dive was made on the same course to intercept and identify. The letter of the day was sent and answered incorrectly.

'Q/502 Sqn at once closed in and came up astern at 500 yards range. The aircraft was then identified as an FW 200. Q/502 proceeded to close from astern and on the port side of enemy aircraft. Enemy aircraft commenced to climb. At 250 to 300 yards, captain instructed second pilot [Flg Off A T Brock] on the front gun to open fire. The first three bursts of tracer appeared to pass the port side of the aircraft.

'At 200 to 300 yards enemy aircraft commenced to fire with tracer from a position on top of the fuselage aft of the mainplane. Q/502 was unable to close the range and instructions were given to the second pilot to continue firing. He then fired a series of short bursts and tracer appeared to enter the enemy aircraft amidships on the port side. Enemy aircraft then opened fire from a second position on the port side of the fuselage while maintaining fire with his top gun. Four black objects were then seen approaching. These passed underneath and were followed by explosions, three in the cockpit (one between the Captain's legs) and one in the fuselage by the pyrotechnics. The explosions caused injury by shrapnel to the Captain's arm and a fire was started among the pyrotechnics. The navigator went aft and with the second radio operator successfully extinguished the fire.

'One enemy bullet entered the front turret through the Perspex close to the second pilot's head. The second pilot continued to fire bursts at enemy aircraft which appeared to enter enemy aircraft amidships. At this time the pilot was endeavouring to gain on enemy aircraft in order to bring rear

Fw 200C-3 Wk-Nr 0046 F8+EL of 3./KG 40 developed a technical defect while being flown by Leutnant Robert Maly on 9 July 1941 and suffered 30 per cent damage upon landing at Cognac. Seen here after it was repaired, Wk-Nr 0046 featured a sunken ship tally on its rudder like a number of Condors from this period

guns to bear without having to turn away and so rapidly widen the range. Enemy aircraft then entered cloud.

'At 0816 hrs the starboard engine of Q/502 began to show signs of overheating and the Captain decided to break off combat and turn back towards the convoy. At 0820 hrs, the starboard engine then began to overheat rapidly, petrol pressure dropped and a slight fire started round the engine with the escape of glycol. With the leading escort vessel of the convoy four to five miles ahead and the height at 1000 ft, the starboard engine lost further power and the Captain gave the order "Prepare to land in the sea". After the starboard engine had stopped and the height could not be maintained, bombs and pyrotechnics were jettisoned. Aircraft still lost height and SOS was signalled to leading vessel by Aldis lamp. The aircraft struck the water 800 to 1000 yards from the leading escort vessel at 0825 hrs. Dinghies were launched and crew held on until rescued. Before sinking, the aircraft was found to have several bullet holes along the starboard side of the fuselage and there were six bullet holes in one of the dinghies.'

This was the first confirmed aerial victory for a Condor. The following day (18 July) I./KG 40 suffered another serious loss. Hauptmann Fritz Fliegel and his crew had taken off in Fw 200C-3 Wk-Nr 0043, coded F8+AB, and it is believed that they had found convoy OB 346, which had departed Liverpool four days earlier bound for Freetown. One of the pilots on the FCS vessel HMS *Maplin* wrote in his diary for that date;

'While I was having my breakfast and Bob [Lt Bob Everett] was in the aircraft, a Condor arrived and started to circle the convoy at much closer range. We were tempted to fire off but restrained ourselves as he didn't attack. He continued to circle the convoy at varying stages for about an hour before retiring in a southerly direction. We had scarcely lost sight of him in the distance when there was a tremendous rumpus aft, where they had spotted another Condor at sea-level, approaching the convoy point blank and already close in. We immediately fired Bob off in a Hurricane but before he had time to turn round and close with the Condor, it had dropped a stick of bombs across another ship and set the bridge on fire.'

Visible on the nose of SG+KS are the last two digits of its Wk-Nr, 0043. Photographed here during post-production test flights whilst still with Focke-Wulf Flugzeugbau, this aircraft later became C-3/U2 F8+AB of I./KG 40. On 18 July 1941 the Condor received a direct hit by AA, which ripped off its starboard wing. The lucky shot was fired by either the armed merchantmen SS *Norman Prince* or by SS *Pilar de Larrinaga*. Hauptmann Fritz Fliegel and his crew were killed when the aircraft cartwheeled into the Atlantic

Before the Hurricane could attack, Bob Everett watched as a segment of the Condor's starboard wing broke off. The aeroplane had received a direct hit by AA fire, which ripped off its wing (another example of the Condor's structural weakness). The lucky shot was fired by either the armed merchantmen SS *Norman Prince* (which was sunk by U-156 on 29 May 1942) or by SS *Pilar de Larrinaga*. The Condor cartwheeled into the Atlantic, taking its crew with it. I./KG 40 had lost its most senior officer to date, and the second *Ritterkreuz* holder in a month.

Fliegel was replaced by Hauptmann Edmund Daser (left), formerly *Staffelkäpitan* of 1./KG 40 and the *Ergäzungsstaffel*/KG 40. He is seen here with Major Edgar Petersen

Fliegel was replaced by another experienced Condor pilot, Hauptmann Edmund Daser, who had in turn succeeded Hauptmann Roman Steszyn as *Staffelkäpitan* of 1./KG 40 on 20 July 1940. In April 1941 Daser had taken command of the *Ergänzungsstaffel* to train new Condor crews. Daser, aged 33, had joined the military in 1932 and flown with II./KG 154 and II./KG 157. In March 1939 he had been attached to the Focke-Wulf Flugzeugbau as a pilot, where he doubtless gained much experience on the Condor prior to being posted to 1./KG 40 in April 1940. Having met with considerable success, Daser had been awarded the *Ritterkreuz* in February 1941 – the third I./KG 40 pilot to receive this decoration, and a month before his predecessor. In September 1941 Daser was replaced by Hauptmann Roman Dawczynski, who had succeeded Fliegel as *Staffelkapitän* of 2./KG 40.

As if the loss of Fliegel was not bad enough, on 23 July 1941 Oberfeldwebel Heinrich Bleichert from *Stab* I./KG 40 was shot down by a No 233 Sqn

On 23 July 1941 Oberfeldwebel Heinrich Bleichert from *Stab* I./KG 40 was shot down by a No 233 Sqn Hudson Mk V flown by Plt Off Ron Down while attacking convoy OG 69 off Achil Head, on the west coast of Ireland. Bleichert managed to ditch, with the only fatality being the meteorological forecaster. Bleichert and his remaining five crewmen were all captured

The crew of Fw 200C-3 F8+EK of 2./KG 40 run its starboard engines up on a wet ramp at Bordeaux-Mérignac in 1941. The aeroplane appears to be devoid of weaponry in either its dorsal turret or ventral gondola

Hudson flown by Flg Off Ron Down while attacking convoy OG 69 off Achil Head. Bleichert managed to ditch, with the only fatality being the meteorological forecaster. Bleichert and his remaining five crew were all captured. The following day the *Staffelkapitän* of 1./KG 40, Hauptmann Konrad Verlohr, failed to return from a mission west of Ireland. He was the second I. *Gruppe* Executive Officer to be lost in just six days.

July 1941 had definitely seen a change in fortunes. In addition to the losses and poor serviceability (on 26 July I./KG 40 reported a strength of 25 aircraft, but only five were serviceable), not a single ship was confirmed as being sunk by I./KG 40 for the entire month. In the first two months of 1941 Condors participated in the sinking of some 39 vessels, with a further 17 credited to the unit from March to July 1941. Just four were sunk or badly damaged by Fw 200s during the last five months of the year. The crews of 3./KG 40 reported encountering shipping 11 times during July, but their only success was the shooting down of the No 502 Sqn Whitley on the 17th.

At about this time, owing to the lack of serviceable aircraft, improved defences against low-flying Condor attacks and losses, it was decreed that in order to reduce the risk being posed to crews, low-level attacks should be abandoned by I./KG 40. Targets were now to be approached from higher altitudes instead. This resulted in a modification to the existing Fw 200C-3 to C-3/U2 standard, which entailed removing the 20 mm cannon in the nose and replacing it with the superlative Carl Zeiss-manufactured Lotfernrohr (Lotfe) 7D bombsight, which provided outstanding accuracy from altitude.

Thus, further out into the Atlantic, the Condors of I./KG 40 continued to be a menace to Allied shipping, generally shadowing convoys and radioing locations to enable U-boat attacks, while staying away from ever-improving Allied defences and retaining the ability to attack from altitude when it was prudent to do so.

By now, the threat of the Condors had at last forced the Allies to come up with various ideas to defend against them. First was the Holman Projector, which used high-pressure steam from the ship's boilers to throw grenades in front of an attacker. Then came the Type E System, better known as the Parachute Aerial Cable, which used a rocket to fire a 600 ft cable above the ship. At the top of the projectile's trajectory, a parachute would open, under which was a small bomb. Finally, there was the 'Condor Trap Ship', which pretended to be an unarmed merchantman but was in

This Condor, believed to be F8+GL of 3./KG 40, flown by Oberleutnant Franz Vuellers, returned to Cognac on 13 August 1941 with a Parachute Aerial Cable (PAC) device attached to its starboard wing. This was one of a number of *ad hoc* anti-air weapons that were urgently devised by the Admiralty in an attempt to defend merchantmen from aerial attacks. As show here, these makeshift weapons all proved to be dismal failures, never downing a Condor or seriously interfering with KG 40's anti-shipping attacks

Oberleutnants Vuellers (left, wearing the officer's visor cap) and Bernhard Jope, *Staffelkapitän* of 3./KG 40, take a closer look at the PAC device

fact a 'wolf in sheep's clothing', armed with two six-inch guns and some light AA weaponry. Known as an ocean boarding vessel and christened HMS *Crispin*, the ship never had the chance to prove its worth for on 3 February 1941 it was sunk by U-107.

What was needed to counter the Condor were fighter aircraft. As has been mentioned earlier, by the time Hauptmann Fritz Fliegel was shot down on 18 July 1941, FCS vessels had started to enter service. Five merchantmen were converted (*Pegasus*, *Ariuani*, *Springbank*, *Patia* and *Maplin*) to allow them to 'fire and forget' Fairy Fulmar Is or Sea Hurricanes of 804 Naval Air Squadron (NAS). Having driven off or shot down the Condor, the naval aviators would either head for a friendly airfield or ditch near the convoy they were protecting.

The first successful interception occurred on 11 May 1941 when Sub-Lt F M Harvey and Leading Airman D Sykes in Fulmar N4072 were launched at a Condor that then turned away, the Fulmar landing in Iceland. However, the first and only victory for an FCS fighter went to Lt Bob Everett of 804 NAS on 3 August 1941. Having witnessed from the air the wing of Hauptmann Fritz Fliegel's Condor being shot off on 18 July before he could get into position to fire, Everett, as part of convoy OG 70/SL 81, was scrambled from the *Maplin* to intercept a Condor that he duly claimed to

A Hurricane IA mounted on the 23-metre long rocket catapult rail on a CAM ship in 1941. Hurricanes were loaded onto the ship using cranes, and each CAM ship had two such aircraft, with one ready to launch and the other on deck. The Hurricane pilot would have to climb a nine-metre ladder to reach the cockpit, and he would sit strapped in for a shift lasting two hours. The catapult was angled toward the starboard bow, the fighter sitting atop a trolley that was accelerated forward by a series of three-inch rockets

have shot down before he bailed out of his Sea Hurricane and was quickly picked up. Despite his claim, the Fw 200 pilot managed to make it back to France, where his aeroplane was then destroyed in a crash-landing, killing two crewman and injuring the weather forecaster. Bob Everett was quite rightly awarded the Distinguished Service Order for his deed.

However, the full effectiveness of the FCSs was limited. Only eight launches were made against Condors, and just one of these resulted in the eventual destruction of the attacker. Furthermore, two of the five ships were sunk and one badly damaged. *Patia* fell victim to an He 111 of 1./KG 26 (which was then itself shot down) while on sea trials off the Northumberland coast on 27 April 1941, *Springbank* was sunk on 27 September 1941 by U-201 and *Ariguani* was badly damaged by U-83 on 26 October 1941.

FCSs were supplanted by CAM ships – normal freighters fitted with a catapult, onto which was mounted a Hurricane – from the spring of 1941. Some 19 vessels were initially earmarked for conversion, and Fighter Command allocated 60 Hurricanes to the Merchant Ship Fighter Unit (MSFU). The first converted vessel to sail was the *Michael E*, which left for New York on 28 May 1941, only to be sunk by U-108 five days later. Just one launch was made in 1941, by former Battle of Britain pilot Plt Off George Varley from the *Empire Foam* on 1 November 1941, and he successfully drove off a Condor. The CAM ships soldiered on until July 1943, by which time they had been replaced by aircraft carriers. CAM ship Hurricanes achieved just one Condor kill when, on 1 November 1942, Flg Off Norman Taylor (another former Battle of Britain pilot), flying off the *Empire Heath*, shot down the Fw 200 commanded by Oberleutnant Arno Gross of 7./KG 40.

The most effective Allied defensive measure of 1941 was the introduction of the escort carrier HMS *Audacity*, which carried six Martlets of 802 NAS. One of the first pilots to fly from the vessel was Sub-Lt Eric 'Winkle' Brown;

'I was a young temporary probationary Sub-Lt RNVR and served on HMS *Audacity*, Britain's first escort carrier, on Atlantic convoy protection in 1941. After a short but highly successful operational tour, *Audacity* was torpedoed and sunk on 21 December 1941. At least four Fw 200 Condors had been accounted for by then, as well as a number of U-boats spotted by *Audacity*'s Wildcats and despatched by the convoy's escort group.'

Three Condors can be positively attributed to aircraft flying from *Audacity*. On 21 September, during convoy OG 74, Sub-Lts Norris Patterson and Graham Fletcher shot down Leutnant Georg Schaffranek of 3./KG 40 – there were no survivors after the Condor's tail was shot off in the initial attack. The next engagement came on 8 November during convoy OG 76 when Eric Brown shot down the

This is believed to be Oberleutnant Karl Krüger of 3./KG 40, whose Fw 200 was shot down by a Martlet flown by Sub-Lt Eric 'Winkle' Brown of 802 NAS on 8 November 1941. Brown was flying from the escort carrier HMS *Audacity* at the time, defending convoy OG 74

Oberleutnant Hans-Joachim Hase of 3./KG 40 was the pilot of the last Fw 200 to be downed by 802 NAS flying from *Audacity*, Sub-Lts 'Jimmy' Sleigh and Bertie Williams being credited with its destruction on 19 December. Although the aeroplane was successfully ditched, there were no survivors

Condor flown by Oberleutnant Karl Krüger of 3. *Staffel*. Minutes earlier the Fw 200's gunners had killed 802 NAS's CO, Lt Cdr John Wintour, Again there were no survivors. The last confirmed kill occurred just two days before the sinking of *Audacity* by U-751 on 21 December, as Sub-Lt 'Jimmy' Sleigh later reported;

'A Condor was sighted by a lookout to the east of the convoy about 15 miles away on the port quarter flying at a very low level. Two Wildcats were scrambled at around 1130 hrs – myself and Bertie Williams, my No 2. Weather was clear with broken cloud. The Condor was on a course for France, having no doubt turned for home when the carrier was seen turning into wind. A long chase ensued as the Wildcats did not have much speed advantage. We eventually caught it some 60 miles later and then took another 40 miles to shoot it down! This was due to a gun stoppage. After our first quarter attacks all guns in both aircraft jammed – a situation that was normally rectified by re-cocking the guns from the cockpit. After much re-cocking, only one gun in my aircraft could be made to fire, and in the meantime the Condor was still hell bent for home, flying at 20 ft above the water.

'I decided to have a go at a head-on attack – the Condor was about 30 ft above the sea by now and I was at ten feet. It took another 20 miles to get into position, and at a closing speed of about 500 knots I opened fire with my one gun at maximum range. Ten seconds later the Condor burst into flames and I turned upwards, collecting in the process a stub aerial and 30 ft of Condor wire which got caught up in the aircraft's arrester hook. If the Condor had not taken avoiding action I would have missed him. After the attack the Condor ditched and settled into the water and I saw one man climb out on to the wings, and he waved.'

There were no survivors from Oberleutnant Hans-Joachim Hase's crew. Hase had been awarded the *Ehrenpokal* (Honour Goblet) less than two weeks earlier.

Fw 200C-3/U4 Wk-Nr 0074 F8+GH was photographed at Athens-Eleusis in the late summer of 1941, this aircraft being one of six Condors sent by I./KG 40 to Greece on 26 August to serve with *Kommando* Petersen. The latter unit had been formed to fly anti-shipping missions over the Gulf of Suez. On 5 September F8+GH, flown by Oberleutnant Horst Neumann of 1./KG 40, crashed into the Mediterranean between the island of Fleves and Cape Sounio shortly after taking off from Eleusis on an armed reconnaissance flight, killing the crew

MEDITERRANEAN DIVERSION

In the summer of 1941 I./KG 40 moved away from its usual operating area when *Kommando* Petersen was formed to fly anti-shipping missions over the Gulf of Suez, the Suez Canal and the northern part of the Red Sea, under the control of X. *Fliegerkorps*. Six Condors were sent to Greece at the end of August, together with nine He 111s believed to be from 8./KG 40 (possibly with some from 7./KG 40 as well). The He 111s, commanded by Hauptmann Robert Kowalewski, *Kommandeur* of III./KG 40 since July 1941 and prior to that *Kommandeur* of the torpedo unit II./KG 26, arrived from Soesterberg on 26 August 1941 and were attached to KG 26, apparently for torpedo operations. Coincidentally, it was at about this time that Fw 200s were also being considered for use as torpedo-bombers, so that is possibly why KG 40 was in Greece.

The *Kommando* arrived at Athens-Eleusis on 26 August 1941, although Major Edgar Petersen was soon recalled to Germany to be Director of Research at Rechlin, with special responsibility for the Heinkel He 177. He was replaced by Oberst Dr Georg Pasewaldt, formerly *Kommandeur* of II./KG 40, who then became KG 40's new *Kommodore*, but only until December 1941.

Kommando Petersen flew approximately six sorties a night to the Suez/Red Sea for a very limited period, possibly during 2-10 September, after which the Condors returned to France – the He 111s had flown back to Soesterberg on 8 September. During the *Kommando's* brief existence it is believed that Leutnant Rudolf Mayr attacked the SS *City of Auckland* at 2127 hrs on 3 September but inflicted no damage. However, losses did occur. On 5 September the Condor flown by Oberleutnant Horst Neumann of 1./KG 40 crashed into the Mediterranean between the island of Fleves and Cape Sounio shortly after taking off from Eleusis on an armed reconnaissance flight, killing the crew. An He 111 flown by Feldwebel Werner Titz of 8./KG 40 was shot down during a conventional bombing attack on Abu Sueir, in Egypt, the following day, the aircraft falling victim to South African pilot Lt Eric Watkinson in a No 94 Sqn Hurricane. Titz and his crew of three were all captured.

Although 1941 had started with a bang for I./KG 40, it ended with a whimper. Because of the new tactics forced on the unit, the number of ships it was now sinking had dropped dramatically. Indeed, the SS *Tunisia* on 4 August, SS *Empire Hurst* on 11 August, SS *Walmer Castle* on 21 September and SS *Sarastone* on 29 October were the only sinkings directly attributed to Condors in the final five months of the year.

Encounters with Coastal Command continued, however, with the RAF reporting 13 between August and November, but none from December 1941 through to the end of April 1942. The first clash between a Condor and the newly arrived long-range Consolidated B-24 Liberator (serving with No 120 Sqn) was reported on 4 October 1941, and another running battle between a Sunderland, captained by Flg Off Henry Bailey of No 95 Sqn, and a Condor flown by Feldwebel Kurt Hinze of 3./KG 40 occurred on 14 November 1941. The Sunderland's rear gunner, Sgt Terry McCorry, was killed and the flying boat damaged, with the Condor escaping unscathed. The last casualty for the year occurred on 21 December when Oberleutnant Herbert Schreyer's Fw 200C-3/U4 from 1./KG 40 crashed at Ramales, in Spain, killing the crew.

The lessons of the year had not been lost on the Luftwaffe and, in particular, the outgoing *Fliegerführer Atlantik* himself, Generaleutnant Martin Harlinghausen, who was recuperating from wounds received on an operational flight on 13 October 1941. In January 1942 he was reported as saying, 'Because of the strong defences, Focke-Wulf aircraft can no longer carry out bombing attacks on Atlantic convoys'. Things were changing for the Condor's operational future – a future that would last only another two-and-a-half years.

CHAPTER THREE

1942 – CHANGES

From the start of 1942 the U-boat campaign rapidly escalated following the USA's entry into the war (the early months of operations off American's eastern seaboard were called the 'Second Happy Time' by U-boat crews). I./KG 40 quickly became involved in shadowing Allied convoys, but there were changes afoot for the unit.

Generalleutnant Martin Harlinghausen was replaced by General Ulrich Kesser as *Fliegerführer Atlantik* – Generalmajor Wolfgang von Wild had been covering for Harlinghausen because of the wounds the latter had received in October 1941. Oberst Dr Georg Pasewaldt was replaced as *Kommodore* by Oberst Karl Mehnert, who would himself be replaced in July 1942 by Oberstleutnant Martin Vetter, an experienced anti-shipping pilot who had been awarded the *Ritterkreuz* in May 1940 with II./KG 26.

In March 1942 Hauptmann Edmund Daser's I./KG 40 moved north to Trondheim-Værnes, in Norway, in support of the northern U-boat war and attacks against Arctic convoys (Daser would be replaced by Major Karl Henkelmann in July 1942 when Daser followed Petersen to Rechlin). Before that, Major Robert Kowalewski's III./KG 40 had begun converting to the Condor at Bordeaux-Mérignac, starting with Oberleutnant Rudolf Graeber's 7. *Staffel* at the end of October 1941. Once fully transitioned, 7./KG 40 joined I./KG 40 at Trondheim-Værnes in January 1942. 8./KG 40, commanded by Hauptmann Karl Kahra, converted at Rennes between January and March 1942, finally followed by Hauptmann Franz

Fw 200C-3 F8+DH of 1./KG 40 sits in the snow at Trondheim-Værnes in early 1942. Like many early Condors assigned to I./KG 40, this aircraft was christened after a planet, star or constellation – in this case *Deneb*, after the brightest star in the constellation Cygnus

This close-up of the nose of an Fw 200C-4 reveals the *A-Stand* FW 19 dorsal turret equipped with a 20 mm MG 151/20 cannon. The *D-Stand* ventral gondola has also been upgraded through the fitment of a 13 mm MG 131 heavy machine gun. Finally, the bulge on the underside of the gondola houses a highly effective Lotfe 7D bombsight, which replaced the crude Revi bombsight in the C-4. Focke-Wulf Flugzeugbau built 107 C-4s between March 1942 and May 1943

Hauptmann Karl Kahra (facing the camera in the lifejacket) was *Staffelkapitän* of 8./KG 40 until he was killed in an accident shortly after taking off from Rennes on 11 April 1942

Brey's 9./KG 40 at Orleans-Bricy from the end of April 1942. A number of III./KG 40 aircrew adept in torpedo operations transferred to KG 26 at this time.

Condor numbers were, at last, higher than ever, but the aircraft was still suffering from poor serviceability. For example, on 30 April 1942 III./KG 40 reported having 20 aircraft on strength but only six were combat ready.

Fw 200 losses began early in the year. On 2 January Oberfeldwebel Herbert Fahje of 3./KG 26 was forced to ditch in the Ria de Camarinas, off the southeast coast of Spain, following technical problems, and Oberfeldwebel Werner Bornefeld of 1./KG 40 was shot down by the corvette HMS *Genistra* west of Ireland on 31 January, resulting in the death of the entire crew. Coastal Command recorded just one encounter with Condors during the first five months of the year, however, and just three more Fw 200s, in addition to Oberfeldwebel's Bornefeld's aircraft, were lost in action in the same period.

On 21 February Leutnant Heinz Schwinkendorf of 3./KG 40 failed to return, whilst on 1 May Oberleutnant Siegfried Gall became III./KG 40's first combat loss when his Condor was shot down off Cape St Vincent by the ASW trawler HMS *Imperialist* – Gall and his crew managed to return via Spain. Finally, Oberleutnant Karl Thiede of 7./KG 40 and his crew, who had been forced to ditch in Storsdalsfjord due to technical problems on 22 February, disappeared over the Atlantic during a mission on 9 May. The aircraft Thiede ditched on 22 February, Fw 200C-3 Wk-Nr 0063, was recovered in recent years and is now being restored at the *Deutsches Technikmuseum* in Berlin.

Over the same period, accidents were commonplace, with 13 Condors suffering varying degrees of damage. The most serious incident occurred on 11 April, when Hauptmann Karl Kahra was killed in an accident shortly after taking off from Rennes. His position as *Staffelkapitän* of 8./KG 40 was taken by Hauptmann Walter Rieder, while at the same time Hauptmann Fritz Kunkel assumed command of 9./KG 40. Both were experienced pilots, none more so than Kunkel. On 14 May 1940, while serving with 5./KG 1, his He 111 was shot down by friendly fire. Once he had recovered from his wounds, Kunkel became Adjutant of I./KG 1 and then Adjutant of III./KG 40 by year-end. He flew with 8./KG 40 before being given command of 9./KG 40 in May 1942. Kunkel ended the war flying Ju 88 nightfighters, initially over the Bay of Biscay and finally over Germany.

Compared with the previous year, 1942 proved to be an anti-climax for I./KG 40 and the recently re-equipped III./KG 40, despite

Condors ranging further afield and being kept away from the ever-improving Allied defences. Fw 200s were seen over Spitsbergen, in northern Norway's Svalbard archipelago, from May 1942. Indeed, Oberleutnant Albert Gramkow, *Staffelkapitän* of 1./KG 40, was lost while shadowing convoy PQ 17 off northern Norway on 8 July. At the other end of the Condor's geographical sphere of operations, 9./KG 40's Oberfeldwebel Richard Schöngraf and his crew were killed when their Condor crashed in the Ria de Muros, off northwestern Spain, on 12 July.

That month also saw an unfortunate accident befall KG 40's new *Zerstörer Staffel*, equipped with the Ju 88C-6 (the unit would become V./KG 40 at the end of the year). Although ostensibly a nightfighter, the Ju 88C-6s supplied to the unit were to be used to perform armed reconnaissance and escort missions in daylight over the Bay of Biscay. It was hoped that the heavily armed C-6 could hold its own against Coastal Command fighters, as well as shoot down maritime patrol aircraft. The aeroplane's effectiveness in the latter role was quickly proven on 15 July 1942 when Feldwebel Henny Passier shot down a Wellington of No 311 Sqn. However, in the process of getting used to operating in conjunction with the Fw 200, Hauptmann Karl-Hans Weymar collided with a Condor in his Ju 88C-6 during an air combat training mission on 22 July. Both the Condor, flown by Feldwebel Alfred Praschl of 9./KG 40, and Weymar's aeroplane crashed near Bordeaux-Mérignac, killing all three in the Ju 88 and the eight-man Fw 200 crew.

In August Condors ranged even further afield. On the 7th Oberfeldwebel Alfons Kleinschnittger and his crew from 1./KG 40 were shot down by AA fire, crashing at Danielsenkrateret on Jan Mayen Island, in the Arctic Ocean. One week later the US Army Air Force scored its first victory in the European Theatre of Operations when the aircraft of Oberfeldwebel Fritz Kuhn from 2./KG 40 was intercepted during a mission to Iceland. The details of what happened to the Fw 200 were recounted by Capt Darrell Welch of the 27th Fighter Squadron (FS)/1st Fighter Group (FG);

'On 14 August I heard a large airplane thunder over my Nissen hut billet. I ran outside to see a German four-engined Fw 200 Condor reconnaissance plane flying directly over our base at only a couple of hundred feet of altitude. The flight on alert, led by the squadron commander, Maj Bill Weltman, took off in hot pursuit of the Fw 200. P-39s from the 33rd FS, which was permanently stationed in Iceland, joined in the chase. Maj Weltman's guns jammed, so his wingman, 2Lt Elza Shahan, made the next pass. The Fw 200 had already been set on fire by P-39 pilot 2Lt Joseph Shaffer, who later said he planned to fire his guns at close range and then fly underneath the big plane, but instead he fired and flew through it. As he was firing, the plane exploded in a great blast that rained debris over Reykjavik Bay.'

The Condor fell into the sea eight miles northwest of Grotta Point. There were no survivors.

There was one more loss over Iceland in 1942, when, on 24 October, 2Lts Michael Ingelido

As the night raid on Bordeaux-Mérignac in April 1941 had graphically shown, the Condor was at its most vulnerable on the ground during the early war years. This aerial view of Trondheim-Værnes, showing no fewer than ten Fw 200s from I./KG 40, was taken by an RAF photo-reconnaissance aircraft in July 1942. Although the RAF had very good intelligence on KG 40's activities from this important airfield in Norway, attacks on Trondheim-Værnes were few and far between. Indeed, only two Condors were damaged in the various raids on the base. And this despite the airfield lacking protective revetments or anti-blast barriers for the Fw 200s

An Fw 200C-4 is escorted by Ju 88C-6s from KG 40's new *Zerstörer Staffel* in the summer of 1942, the latter becoming V./KG 40 at year end. Although built to serve as nightfighters, the Ju 88C-6s supplied to the unit performed armed reconnaissance and escort missions in daylight over the Bay of Biscay. The Luftwaffe hoped that the heavily armed C-6 and latterly the R-2 could hold their own against Coastal Command fighters, as well as shoot down maritime patrol aircraft – the Fw 200 struggled to do either

and Thurman Morrison of the 33rd FS shot down the Condor flown by Oberleutnant Heinz Godde of 2./KG 40, which crashed at Kleppatagl, near Surtshellir, northwest of Reykjavik. Some records have stated this aircraft was on loan from the reconnaissance unit 1(F)/120, and flight engineer Unteroffizier Hans Todtenhöfer was indeed from that unit. However, the fact that the Fw 200 was coded F8+EK shows that it was a KG 40 aircraft, even if 1(F)/120 had four Condors on its strength from August to December 1942.

Amongst the KG 40 aircrew in the thick of the action in 1942 was flight engineer and occasional pilot Oberfeldwebel Franz Ziegon of 9. *Staffel*. Having joined the unit in May of that year, he flew his first operational mission with the *Staffelkapitän* of 8./KG 40, Hauptmann Walter Rieder, as his pilot during the afternoon of 30 May. Conducting a 13-hour armed reconnaissance of the Bay of Biscay, the flight was uneventful, even if they were shot at by ships of the Royal Navy. For the next few months Ziegon flew infrequently on similar missions, failing to encounter the enemy on each occasion. This all changed on 17 August, however. While on yet another armed reconnaissance, Ziegon's Condor, flown by his usual pilot, Leutnant Georg Ulrici, stumbled across a No 58 Sqn Whitley flown by Plt Off Ken Clugston near Cape St Vincent, off the southern coast of Portugal. A running battle ensued, the Condor being hit 37 times and the radio operator, Unteroffizier Alfons Kiefer, killed. However, the Whitley was eventually shot down and its entire crew killed. Only the body of Wireless Operator/Air Gunner Sgt Ted Phillipson was recovered, being washed ashore at Cedeira, in Spain.

Ziegon flew three more armed reconnaissance missions in August 1942, and on two of them the Condor came within visual range of the Scilly Isles. Much of September saw him and his crew engaged on trials with the Rostock ASV radar away from Bordeaux-Mérignac, Ziegon's only operational flight coming on the 1st when his crew shadowed a convoy until driven off by a Sunderland of No 201 Sqn flown by Flt Lt George Bunting. Ziegon and his crew eventually returned to Bordeaux-Mérignac at the end of September, after which they flew two armed reconnaissance missions (lasting nearly 11 hours and 11.5 hours, respectively) before heading to Trondheim-Værnes in late October. From here they flew just one 11-hour armed reconnaissance to Iceland and Greenland on 28 October. That same day 3./KG 40's Oberleutnant Rudolf Feldt and his crew failed to return from a similar mission in the same location.

Ziegon's logbook from this period shows a change in task for III./KG 40 from late October. On the 25th an unnamed detachment of Condors moved to Lecce, in southern Italy, from where they undertook flights to North Africa, transporting fuel for the *Afrika Korps*. Initially commanded by Hauptmann Alfred Hemm (who was replaced by Hauptmann Rudolf Mayr when Hemm took command of V./KG 40), the detachment carried out freight duties until mid-February 1943. The Ulrici crew, including Franz Ziegon, arrived at Lecce on 2 December. According to Ziegon's logbook he made no fewer than 52 transport flights before returning to Bordeaux-Mérignac on 15 February 1943.

Oberfeldwebel Alfons Kleinschnittger and his crew from 1./KG 40 were shot down by AA fire, crashing at Danielsenkrateret on Jan Mayen Island, in the Arctic Ocean on 7 August 1942. There were no survivors

With the Atlantic U-boat war continuing and the numbers of Allied ships and, more importantly, Allied aircraft increasing, Condor attrition in 1942, both in combat and due to accidents, had risen. No fewer than 26 aircraft were lost by I. and III./KG 40 throughout the year, the last occurring on 31 December during an audacious mission. In addition to Oberleutnant Dietrich Weber of 2./KG 40 failing to return from shadowing convoy JW 51B somewhere between Norway and Iceland on that date, the Luftwaffe also decided to send 12 aircraft from III./KG 40 to attack Casablanca, in Morocco. Intelligence had reported that eastbound convoy UGS 3 – 39 ships escorted by the US Navy destroyers USS *Wainwright* (DD-419), USS *Mayrant* (DD-402), USS *Rhind* (DD-404), USS *Trippe* (DD-403) and USS *Rowan* (DD-405) – was in harbour, so it was decided to carry out the biggest Condor attack of the war to date.

Eleven aircraft managed to take off from Bordeaux-Mérignac, but three subsequently returned with instrument failure, flight control issues and engine problems. Of the remaining eight, seven attacked between 0303 hrs and 0442 hrs at heights varying between 800 m and 3500 m (2600 ft and 11,500 ft). The Condor crews thought that they had surprised the Allies, reporting a number of hits with two SC 500, 16 SC 250, 19 SBC 50 and four ABB 500 bombs. However, no significant damage was inflicted, and the Condors suffered losses on the way home. Short of fuel, Hauptmann Fritz Hoppe of 8./KG 40 was forced to land at San Pablo airport in Seville, where his Condor was interned by Spanish authorities, while Oberleutnant Rudolf Graeber of 7./KG 40 radioed at 0805 hrs that he was south of Huelva, in southern Spain, two of his engines had failed and he had been unable to attack. During his last transmission Graeber stated that he was landing in southern Spain. In June 1943 the body of one of his gunners was washed ashore – no trace of the remaining six crewmen was found.

It had been a year of mixed fortunes for the Condors of KG 40, with the *Geschwader* expanding and at the same time operating much further afield on transport tasks as well as in its normal maritime roles. However, there were still insufficient numbers of Fw 200s, and aircraft lost (both operationally and non-operationally) were still proving hard to make good. It was hoped that replacing the Condor with the He 177 would see a change in fortunes for KG 40, but with ongoing development problems continuing to beset the Heinkel bomber, it was becoming increasingly clear that this would not be the case.

Flight engineer and occasional pilot Oberfeldwebel Franz Ziegon joined 9./KG 40 in May 1942 and saw considerable action with the *Staffel* into 1943. Indeed, he flew missions from Bordeaux-Mérignac, Trondheim-Værnes and Lecce during this period

A Condor pilot (left) and co-pilot photographed during a long-range patrol over the Atlantic. Despite the heavy flight gear and lifejackets, Fw 200 crews knew that in the event of a water landing they were well beyond the range of German air-sea rescue. In most cases, their only hope of survival rested with the vessels they had just attacked

CHAPTER FOUR

1943 – BEGINNING OF THE END

This aircraft is believed to be Fw 200C-3 Wk-Nr 0095 F8+DH of 1./KG 40, photographed during a resupply flight in North Africa in late 1942 – note the white Mediterranean theatre band on the rear fuselage. Wk-Nr 0095 was lost operating with KGrzbV 200 during the Stalingrad airlift on 19 January 1943

Almost simultaneously with III./KG 40 providing support in North Africa, Condors were rushed eastwards to help with the resupply effort for the encircled German 6th Army at Stalingrad. The aircraft used formed KGzbV 200, commanded by Major Hans-Jürgen Willers of 11./KG 40, the *Staffelführer* for the Fw 200s being Oberleutnants Franz Schulte-Vogelheim and, latterly, Karl-Heinz Hausknecht of I./KG 40.

Unlike the flights in North Africa, the missions flown on the eastern front were highly eventful due to the combination of Soviet AA fire and very poor weather. The first aircraft losses occurred on 10 January 1943, when Oberfeldwebel Werner Brune's Condor was destroyed in a landing accident and Oberfeldwebel's Eugen Reck's Fw 200 went missing. The last reported loss was Oberfeldwebel Karl Wittmann's aeroplane on 30 January, which was also listed as missing. The ultimately unsuccessful attempt to keep the 6th Army supplied with provisions from the air at Stalingrad cost KG 40 five Condors, with another three aeroplanes suffering varying degrees of damage.

Understandably, Fw 200 operations over the Atlantic were much reduced in January 1943. In fact, Coastal Command did not encounter any Condors between 22 November 1942 and 26 February 1943. Another aircraft

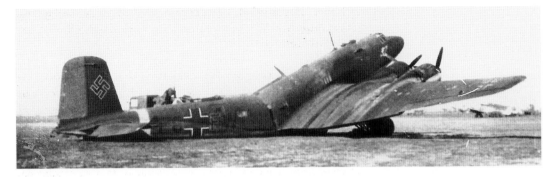

from 8./KG 40, coded F8+HS, landed at San Pablo airport in Seville, on 1 January 1943, where it too was interned alongside Hauptmann Fritz Hoppe's F8+AS, which had flown in short on fuel the previous day. The first Fw 200 to be lost in action was the 7./KG 40 aeroplane of Leutnant Ernst Rabolt on 12 March, the Condor being intercepted by four Beaufighters of No 248 Sqn. This was the second time an Fw 200 had fallen victim to heavily armed land-based long-range Allied fighters, for on 17 September 1942 Oberfeldwebel Konrad Bär's 8./KG 40 machine had crashed near Belle Isle, off the Brittany coast, after being intercepted by eight Beaufighters from No 235 Sqn. Putting up stiff resistance, Bär's crew (five of whom were wounded and two killed) managed to shoot one of the Coastal Command aircraft down before ditching. However, there were no Beaufighters lost during the downing of Rabolt's aircraft, and no survivors from the Fw 200.

March 1943 was a particularly bad month for the Condor, for in addition to Leutnant Rabolt's loss, another Fw 200 was destroyed in a takeoff accident at Trondheim-Værnes, a third was mistakenly shot down by German AA fire west of Royan and a fourth was all but written off in a crash-landing at Cognac due to engine failure. There were also two more combat losses, the first of which involved the Fw 200C-4 captained by Oberleutnant Erich Schlebach on 19 March. Although flying a 2./KG 40 aircraft, he was assigned to KGzbV 200 and subordinate to III./KG 40. Schlebach was shadowing convoy KMS 11 that day, 64 merchantmen and 20 escorts having set sail from the Clyde on 14 March bound for the Algerian port of Bone.

One of the escorts was the Free French sloop *Savorgnan de Brazza*, captained by Commandant André Jubelin. In his book *The Flying Sailor*, published in 1953, Jubelin records being awoken by an unidentified aircraft, thought possibly to be a B-17 Flying Fortress, even though he, an experienced naval aviator, thought otherwise;

'Emerging from cloud cover just sufficiently to take a bearing, a superb four-engined bomber was coming straight for us. "Range 2000 [m], 1800 [m]" announced the telemeter operator. Facing the machine, it was impossible to make out its markings. Truth be told, it might easily have been mistaken for a Flying Fortress, but that was not the reason I delayed giving the order to open fire. I had so often performed the operation of attacking vessels from an aircraft that I believed I knew exactly what the pilot was thinking. One is never so nervous as when, after getting within range, one is keeping lookout for the first AA bursts. Paradoxical as it may appear, one's anxiety is dissipated as soon as fire is opened.

"'1600 [m], 1400 [m].'"

While flying with 1./KGzbV 200, Fw 200C-3 Wk-Nr 0049 F8+FW suffered a fuselage breakage following a heavy landing at Saporoshje during the Stalingrad airlift in early 1943. Its pilot, Oberfeldwebel Werner Böck, was subsequently reported missing during an Atlantic patrol on 24 March 1943

'It is to the seaman's advantage to wait, though not unreasonably long. The gunlayers see their target better and the weapons are less likely to jam at the first discharge.

'"1200 [m]."

'"Fire!" Thirty-seven guns of all calibres spat flame. A sheet of red tracer converged on the aircraft. In less than ten seconds an incandescent sphere appeared at the juncture of the right wing, expanded and burst. The machine caught fire and dived out of control. At an altitude of 150 ft a man sprang out of it, but before his parachute could open he crashed into the water almost at the same time the huge plane followed in a vast fountain of spray. At the point of impact, petrol continued to burn, sending out thick clouds of smoke. Wreckage floated to the surface. A tremendous cheer broke out aboard except on the bridge.'

Some of the sailors were convinced that they had shot down a Flying Fortress, but in amongst the wreckage, which included a fuel tank and a tyre, they recovered a body identified as Feldwebel Walter Fröhlich, who was the Condor's second pilot – incontrovertible proof that the French gunners had indeed shot down the correct aircraft.

André Jubelin also confirmed in his book that from 19 March onwards Condors constantly harassed the convoy;

'On the following day, two Condors attempted to bomb us and made off after being caught in a tight network of our tracers. Meanwhile, we were approaching Gibraltar. The first day of spring found us about 100 miles off Lisbon, under a sullen sky. The Condors continually harassed the rear of the convoy at a safe distance from our guns. It was flattering evidence of the respect which they had for our armament.

'Towards the middle of the afternoon we were following through our binoculars the attack of a Condor on a large steamer that brought up the rear of the first column of the convoy. The bomber dived through an inferno to launch its bombs, two of which scored hits.'

They had witnessed the attack on the 6000 brt SS *City of Christchurch* west of Lisbon on 21 March, which resulted in KG 40's first confirmed sinking for nearly a year. Two claims were submitted by 7./KG 40, one by the *Staffelkapitän*, Hauptmann Dr Lambert von Konschegg, and the other by Oberleutnant Bernhard Kunisch. The latter pilot and his crew were almost certainly responsible for the successful attack.

The final combat loss of March 1943 was the Fw 200C-4 captained by Oberfeldwebel Werner Böck of 7./KG 40, which was reported missing over the Atlantic on the 24th. Bodies of four crewmen were later washed ashore at San Sebastian, in northern Spain.

With so many casualties in the first three months of the year, KG 40 drastically scaled back its operational flying until the early summer. The next combat loss did not occur until 13 June, and in the intervening three months just one Condor was lost, in a takeoff accident, in April. Coastal Command also reported only a single encounter with an Fw 200 during the same period.

Another possible reason for this inactivity was the reorganisation and re-equipping of KG 40. In September 1942 1./KG 40, commanded by Hauptmann Ernst Pflüger, had moved to Fassberg, in Germany, to start training on the He 177. It was followed in March 1943 by 8./KG 40,

commanded by Hauptmann Walter Rieder. Thus, KG 40's Condor *Staffeln* were a total of four split between Bordeaux-Mérignac and Trondheim-Værnes. Training crews to fly the He 177 (the Condor's anticipated replacement) had started in mid-1942, and despite many ex-Fw 200 pilots being involved the development programme was plagued by problems. It was well behind schedule as a result.

In July 1942 I./KG 50 had been formed at Brandenburg-Briest from parts of 10./KG 40, commanded by Hauptmann Heinrich Schlosser, and the *Geschwader* (in reality just I. *Gruppe*) commanded by Major Kurt Schede. In December 1942 this unit moved to Zaporozhye, in the Soviet Union, with seven He 177s for winter trials, but it quickly became involved in resupplying Stalingrad. Schede was killed on one of the first missions (on 16 January 1943) when, bound for Poliakowka, the aeroplane apparently crashed near Talovoy-Schlucht. There were no survivors. Schlosser then took command of the *Gruppe*, which had lost five aircraft and 28 aircrew (with four more wounded) by the time he led it back to Germany at the end of January.

Once home, I./KG 50 continuing with bombing and then anti-shipping trials, as well as more training. The latter included training with and development of the Henschel Hs 293 anti-shipping glide bomb. Schlosser reported afterwards 'engine fires in the air have been responsible for the loss of five [He 177A-1s], a casualty rate of 26 per cent. Due to the location of the engines to the rear of the pilot, fires are generally not discovered until it is too late'. Chronic engine unreliability was the primary reason why it took the Luftwaffe so long to get the He 177 – the Fw 200's replacement – into operational service, and why the Condor had to soldier on longer than intended.

In June 1943 the Do 217-equipped II./KG 40 started converting to the Messerschmitt Me 410, being re-designated V./KG 2 at this time. On 25 October I./KG 50 duly became II./KG 40, Hauptmann Schlosser handing over command to another former Condor contemporary of his, Major Rudolf Mons. It was not until 21 November 1943 that the He 177 was at last sent into action.

Meanwhile, back over the Atlantic, it was announced that, with effect from 3 June 1943, U-boats would transit the Bay of Biscay in groups of two or three and, if attacked, they were to fight it out on the surface. Pre-empting this, V./KG 40 began to intensify its anti-aircraft missions over the area, and as a result RAF Fighter Command began to fly what was known as 'Instep' patrols – formations usually of four Mosquitoes tasked with restricting attacks on Coastal Command aircraft (*text continues on page 60*)

In 1943 RAF Coastal Command launched an aerial offensive in the Bay of Biscay that seriously hindered KG 40's anti-shipping operations. This dramatic photograph captures the final moments of 7./KG 40's Fw 200C-4 Wk-Nr 0186 F8+ER, flown by Leutnant Ernst Rabolt. Intercepted by four Beaufighters of No 248 Sqn on 12 March 1943, the Condor was quickly despatched. There were no survivors

Having enjoyed early success with KG 40 and its Fw 200s, Hauptmann Heinrich Schlosser was transferred with his *Staffel* (10./KG 40) to the newly formed He 177 unit I./KG 50 in July 1942. He would eventually fly the troublesome He 177 with this unit and be involved in transport missions during the resupply of Stalingrad in 1942-43

COLOUR PLATES

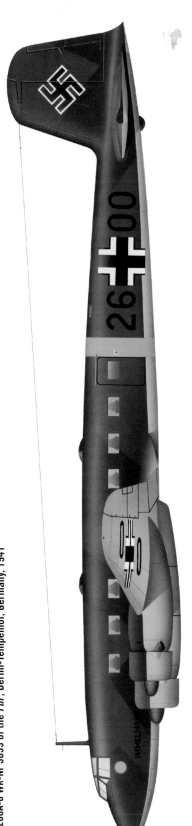

1
Fw 200A-0 Wk-Nr 3099 of the *FdF*, Berlin-Tempelhof, Germany, 1941

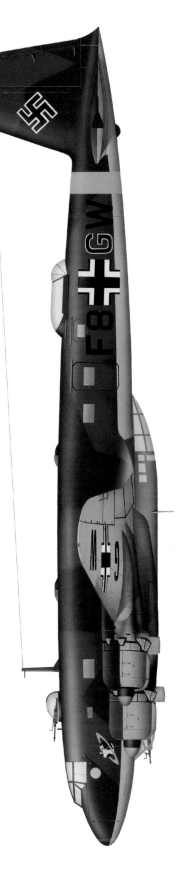

2
Fw 200C-3 Wk-Nr 0034 F8+GW of IV./KG 40 and KGzbV 200, Gumrak, USSR, January 1943

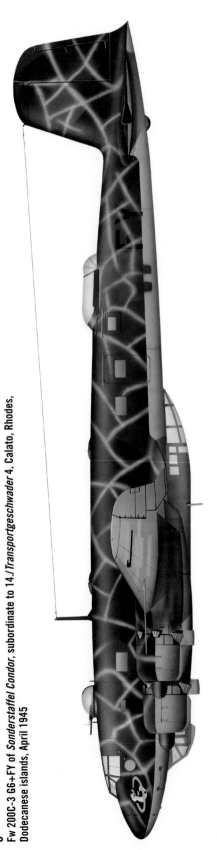

3
Fw 200C-3 G6+FY of *Sonderstaffel Condor*, subordinate to 14./*Transportgeschwader 4*, Calato, Rhodes, Dodecanese islands, April 1945

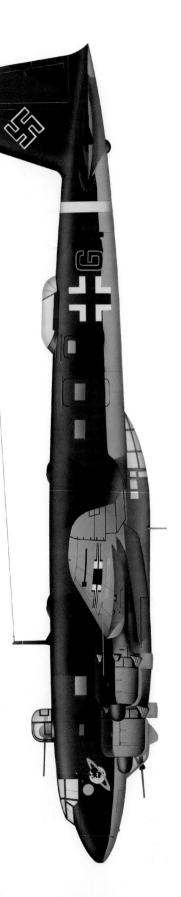

4
Fw 200C-4 F8+GT of 9./KG 40, Lecce, Italy, November 1942

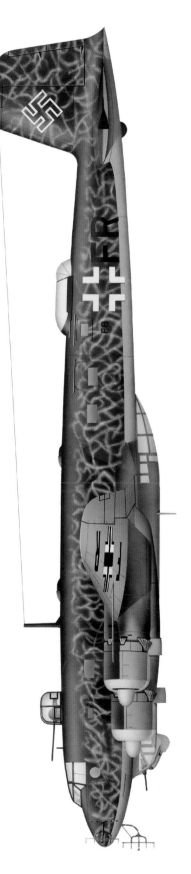

5
Fw 200C-4/U1 Wk-Nr 0176 GC+AE/5 of the *FdF*, Flensburg, Germany, Spring 1945

6
Fw 200C-8 F8+FR of 7./KG 40, Gotenhafen-Hexengrund, Poland, May 1944

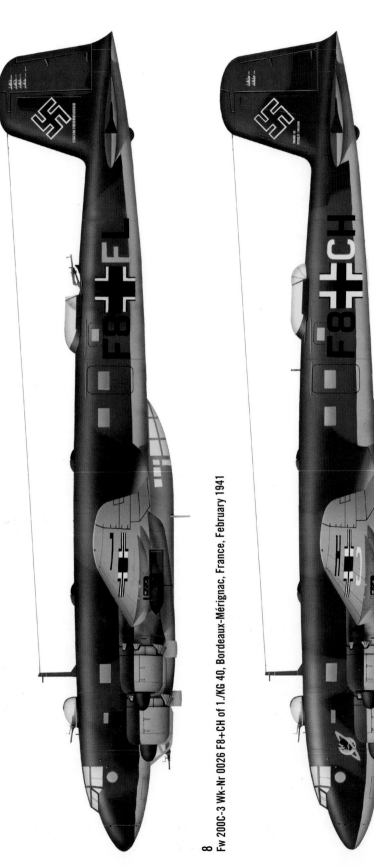

7
Fw 200C-3 Wk-Nr 0046 F8+FL (SG+KV) of 3./KG 40, Cognac, France, November 1941

8
Fw 200C-3 Wk-Nr 0026 F8+CH of 1./KG 40, Bordeaux-Mérignac, France, February 1941

9
Fw 200C-3/U5 Wk-Nr 0095 F8+CD (KE+LT) of *Stab* III./KG 40, Bordeaux-Mérignac, France, autumn 1942

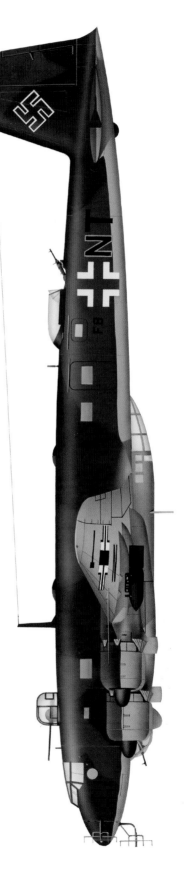

10
Fw 200C-6 Wk-Nr 0214 F8+NT (TA+MP) of 9./KG 40, Bordeaux-Mérignac, France, August 1943

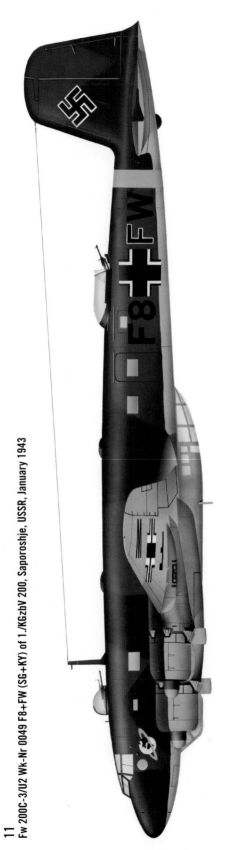

11
Fw 200C-3/U2 Wk-Nr 0049 F8+FW (SG+KY) of 1./KGzbV 200, Saporoshje, USSR, January 1943

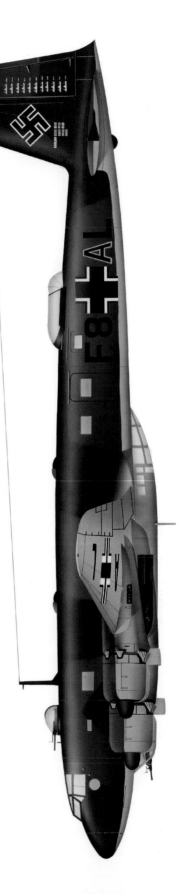

12
Fw 200C-3 F8+AL of 3./KG 40, Bordeaux-Mérignac, France, 1941

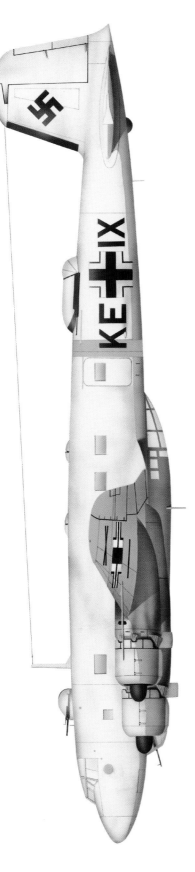

13
Fw 200C-3/U9 WK-Nr 0099 KE+IX of the *FdF*, Berlin-Tempelhof, Germany, 1942

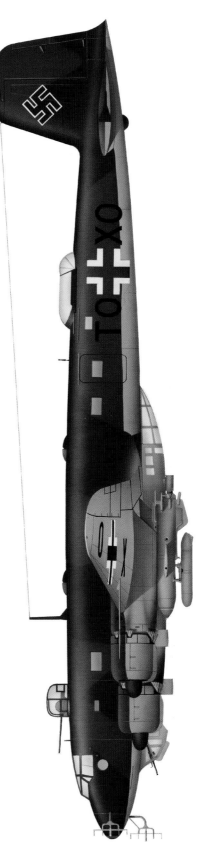

14
Fw 200C-5/FK WK-Nr 0259 TO+XO of III./KG 40, possibly Bordeaux-Mérignac, France, late 1943

56

15
Fw 200C-2 F8+KH of 1./KG 40, Lüneburg, Germany, July 1940

16
Fw 200A-0 Wk-Nr 3098 NK+NM of the *FdF*, Berlin-Tempelhof, Germany, 1941

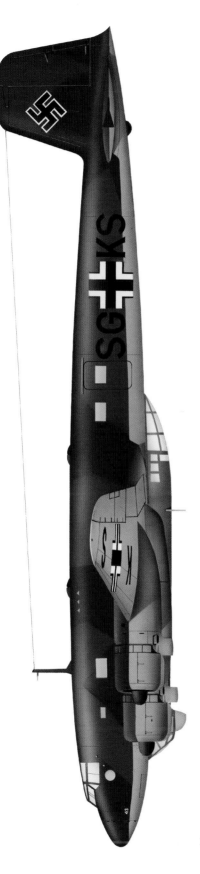

17
Fw 200C-3 Wk-Nr 0043 SG+KS of the Focke-Wulf Flugzeugbau, Bremen, Germany, 1940

18
Fw 200C-1 Wk-Nr 0007 F8+EH of 1./KG 40, Lüneburg, Germany, July 1940

58

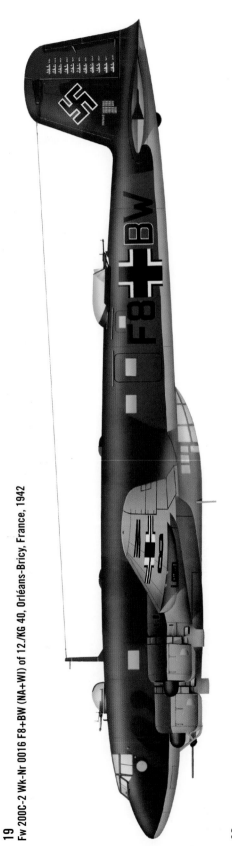

19
Fw 200C-2 Wk-Nr 0016 F8+BW (NA+WI) of 12./KG 40, Orléans-Bricy, France, 1942

20
Fw 200C-5/FK F8+FS of *Transportfliegerstaffel Condor*, Achmer, Germany, May 1945

21
Fw 200C-3 Wk-Nr 0034 of the NII VVS, Chalovskaya, USSR, 1943

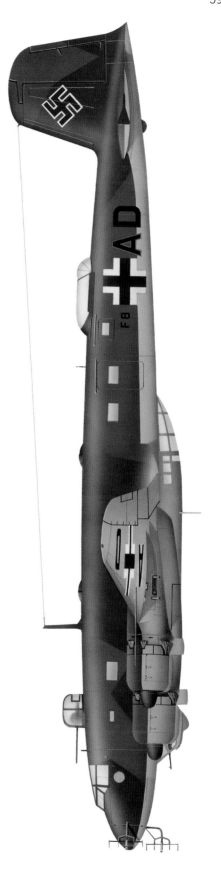

22
Fw 200C-6 Wk-Nr 0218 F8+AD (TA+MT) of *Stab* III./KG 40, Bordeaux-Mérignac, France, August 1943

by maintaining an almost constant presence over the Western Approaches during daylight (Coastal Command did likewise with its Beaufighters). It was inevitable that German losses would start to rise, and on 13 June 1943 Stabsfeldwebel Rudolf Kensok of 7./KG 40 was intercepted by Mosquitoes of No 151 Sqn 400 km west of Bordeaux. The result was the loss of the Condor, shared by the aircraft flown by Flg Off Alistair Boyle and Plt Off Jim Humphries. There were no survivors from the Fw 200's six-man crew.

However, it was not only the RAF that was shooting down Condors, as Oberfeldwebel Georg Abel and his crew from 7./KG 40 found to their cost 11 days later. Sub-Lt Gordon Penny recalled what happened;

'HMS *Battler* was escorting convoy OS 49/KMS 16 and carried six [Fairey] Swordfish of 835 NAS and four [Supermarine] Seafires of 808 NAS, in addition to many Hurricanes destined for Malta which would be flown off by RAF pilots.

'24 June – With only a few minutes to go to sunset, we saw an Fw 200 flying over the convoy and were scrambled [in Seafires]. Lt Constable asked me to lead as he had lost sight of the Fw. We climbed to a position above and astern of the enemy aircraft at about 5000-6000 ft. Constable made a stern attack and I followed. Tracer from the rear gun ceased about halfway through my attack. Breaking away, I saw the port wing of the Fw ablaze. Constable made another attack and followed the Fw nearly to sea level. I returned to *Battler* and landed in the fading light, followed by Constable, who confirmed the kill.'

June 1943 did see the occasional success for Condor crews too, including an unusual one-sided aerial battle. During that month the British Army's Glider Pilot Regiment had began ferrying Horsa gliders, towed behind Handley Page Halifax tugs of No 295 Sqn, to North Africa via Gibraltar. During the morning of 14 June Horsa LG945, flown by SSgt 'Paddy' Conway, got airborne from RAF Portreath, in Cornwall, behind Halifax DK130, flown by WO Bill McCrodden. Earlier that morning two Condors of 7./KG 40, commanded by Oberleutnant Ludwig Progner and Hauptmann Georg Schobert, had taken off from Bordeaux-Mérignac, and at 1106 hrs the Fw 200s intercepted the Horsa and the Halifax.

The glider crew only became aware that they were under attack when tracer rounds appeared between them and the tug, the Condors having positioned themselves either side of the Halifax before opening fire with 20 mm cannon. One of the Army pilots heard a Halifax crewman say over the radio what a dangerous situation they were now in, and then Bill McCrodden called up the Horsa and asked them to 'pull off', which they did. The Horsa eventually ditched 100 miles west of Spain's northwestern coastline. Eleven days later the three Army personnel were rescued by a Spanish fishing boat and landed at Vigo.

Meanwhile, the unequal battle between the two Condors and the Halifax continued at 500 ft above the sea. Almost 20 minutes after the first shot was fired the terminally damaged DK130 was forced to ditch, its demise being credited to Oberleutnant Progner and his crew. Both Condors circled the wallowing Halifax, and it was noted that some of the crew had managed to get into a dinghy. However, the Germans were the last to see the RAF personnel alive, for all six crew are still listed as missing.

THE 'FAITH' ATTACK

The most spectacular success of July 1943 was the attack on convoy 'Faith' by III./KG 40. On 8 July the 16,792 GRT luxury passenger liner *California*, together with the *Duchess of York* (20,021 GRT) and the *Port Fairy* (8072 GRT), left the Clyde for Freetown, in British West Africa, with the destroyer HMS *Douglas* and the frigate HMS *Moyola* as part of the convoy. The *California* was carrying a crew of 316 (including 25 gunners to man its armaments), together with 449 passengers and two Royal Navy signalmen. Built in Glasgow in 1923, it had carried passengers between Glasgow and New York, transferring in 1935 to the Anchor Line. At the outbreak of war the vessel was requisitioned by the Admiralty and converted into an armed merchant cruiser, but from 1942 onward it was used simply as a troopship.

The *Duchess of York* was also built in Scotland, but in 1928 for the Canadian Pacific Steamship Company. Its route was Liverpool to St John's, in Canada, normally via Belfast and Greenock, although it occasionally sailed between New York and Bermuda. At the start of World War 2 the *Duchess of York* took children evacuees to Canada until it was requisitioned by the Admiralty as a troopship and began transporting Canadian soldiers to the UK and RAF aircrew and German PoWs to Canada.

The *Port Fairy* was by no means as exotic as the *California* and *Duchess of York*. Built in 1928 for the Commonwealth and Dominion Line in Wallsend, it was initially employed transporting chilled meat from Australia and New Zealand. At the outbreak of war it was used as an ammunition ship and was nearly lost on 22 October 1940 when, as part of convoy OL 8 from Liverpool to Canada, it collided with HMCS *Margaree* (formerly HMS *Diana*). Although 34 crew were rescued, the warship sank with the loss of its captain, Cdr Joseph Roy, four officers and 136 crew.

The first two days for convoy 'Faith' were uneventful. At 2000 hrs on 10 July the convoy made rendezvous with the Canadian destroyer HMCS *Iroquois* some 500 miles southwest of Land's End, then sailed south, planning to join HMS *Swale* off the Iberian coast 24 hours later. All went without incident until 1850 hrs on Sunday, 11 July, when, 350 miles off the Portuguese coast, an unidentified aircraft was reported in the vicinity. Action stations were ordered and all watertight doors and openings were closed. At 1930 hrs an unidentified aeroplane was sighted from the *California*, approaching from the south. Having levelled with the ship, the aircraft turned away and, gaining height, flew into the sun and was lost to view.

The convoy had been detected by the Luftwaffe, and three Fw 200s from 7./KG 40, commanded by Hauptmann Helmut Liman and Oberleutnants Ludwig Progner and Egon Scherret were sent to investigate. At 2010 hrs they started their attacks, each aircraft dropping four 250 kg bombs from high altitude and with extreme accuracy. Plt Off Peter Dyson was a passenger on the *Duchess of York*;

'There was a series of explosions, all the lights went out and the mirrors shattered. I was unhurt and soon scrambled up and out on to the promenade deck, to see the ship ablaze from amidships to the stern. We had been hit by a string of three bombs dropped by Condors. Both the other ships were also ablaze – the convoy had been wiped out. We discovered years later that we were off the coast of Portugal and thought to be out of range of the Condors, but it was supposed that these had been based in "neutral" Spain, though whether that was actually so I never heard. The other troopship was the *California*, many of the passengers on which were civilians, including a lot of young Irish nuns bound for missions in

The 20,021 GRT troopship *Duchess of York* burns after being attacked by three Fw 200s from 7./KG 40 350 miles off the Portuguese coast during the evening of 11 July 1943. Each aircraft dropped four 250 kg bombs from high altitude with extreme accuracy, this ordnance starting uncontrollable fires in both the *Duchess of York* and the 16,792 grt liner *California*. Part of the ill fated 'Faith' convoy bound for Freetown, in British West Africa, both vessels were eventually sunk by their escorts so as not to present a beacon to German submarines and aircraft. A third troopship, the 8072 GRT *Port Fairy*, was also set on fire during the attack, but the blaze was eventually extinguished and the vessel limped 500 nautical miles to Casablanca

Africa. After the war I discovered that an old school friend was killed on the *California* – he was in the colonial service. The third ship was a "fast cargo liner" and she survived, the fires were extinguished and a destroyer towed her into Casablanca a few days later.

'Although I have forgotten many of the details of my Service life, the events of the next few weeks are as clear as ever, and I could write many pages about them. Briefly, I was picked up by a lifeboat and transferred via scrambling nets to a Royal Navy frigate that picked up several hundred survivors. After two days we docked at Casablanca and we survivors were taken over by the US Army and housed in a tented transit camp.'

The convoy responded with a heavy barrage of AA fire, but the *Duchess of York* was immediately enveloped in flames. The *California* then had a near miss that tore a 100-ft-long hole in its starboard side above the waterline. Soon afterwards the *California* was attacked a second time and hit by two bombs, one of which struck the No 2 hold and the other detonated between the funnel and the bridge. A third bomb went into the sea, although it still blew a hole in the starboard side in the vicinity of No 7 hold. The attacks are summarised by a series of terse radio messages, as follows;

'2110: Attack commenced 41.20N 15.26W. First bombs dropped. Direct hit on *Duchess of York*. Engines crippled.

'2114: Second Fw 200 Green 90 degrees. Bombs dropped. Direct hit *California*. Down in bows. Third Fw circling.

'2120: Third attack. Near miss *Duchess of York*. All three planes circling around.

'2140: Fourth attack. *Port Fairy* near miss.

'2141: Only one aircraft observed.

'2145: Aircraft circling overhead. *Duchess of York* and *California* on fire.'

Able Seaman Charles Aitchison was on watch on the boat deck of the *California* and had spotted the German aircraft – very high and with little or no noise coming from them. Guns had opened fire, but with little effect, and he thought that nothing would happen. He was soon proved wrong;

'Two bombs struck the *Duchess of York* amidships, which immediately lost way and smoke belched out of her. We all deemed this a lucky hit, but hardly had we thought so when a bomb crashed into the *California* on the starboard side aft, apparently just below the waterline. A minute or so later, some of our more optimistic members were suggesting that it was a near hit when a fireman burst on to the deck covered in fine grey dust and blood oozing from his forehead. It was obvious that somewhere near the engine room had been hit.

'I decided that I had better try to rescue some of my belongings, and ran down the various companionways to the working alleyway with the intention of going up for'ard and grabbing one or two of my possessions. When running along this alley, a second bomb smashed into us. I was thrown back in my tracks and a blast of hot air scorched my face. I can remember putting my hand up to my mouth to feel if my teeth were still there. They were. Still thinking of saving my few valuables I tried to go forward when a third bomb hit our side near No 2 Hold. I arrived on the foredeck to find everything around No 2 Hatch in ruins. Some two dozen wounded, too ghastly to describe, were lying there. We dragged them under the cover of the deck, as the planes were circling overhead again. The order to abandon ship had been given some time previous and a few of our lifeboats were in the water.'

According to the captain's report, the *California*'s engines were undamaged in the attack but the steering gear was put out of action and all communication with the bridge was lost except for the engine-room telegraph. However, the real threat was from fire, for, as he reported, 'the whole vessel appeared to be blazing'. After the second hit he ordered the engines to be stopped and the boats lowered. Although at first it was hoped that it might still be possible to save the ship, the fire and heat were so terrific that it was obvious that the situation was hopeless, and the order to abandon ship was given. Of 30 lifeboats on the ship, 17 got away safely as well as a number of rafts. A total of 45 crew and 21 passengers were eventually reported missing and one man subsequently died in hospital.

It was a similar story on the *Duchess of York* – 27 passengers and crew lost their lives. The ship had quickly become a raging inferno and communication between the bridge and the rest of the vessel was impossible, so Capt William Busk-Wood ordered abandon ship. He and his chief engineer were the last to leave at about 2240 hrs.

The attack, from 15,000 ft, was a spectacular success, lasting a little less than 30 minutes. Six attacking runs were made, during which 14 bombs were said to have been dropped – four were direct hits and ten were near misses. The hulk of the *Duchess of York* was still afloat the following morning, and was photographed by the Condor commanded by Hauptmann Paul Husslein of III./KG 40.

The pilot responsible for damaging the only surviving ship of the convoy, the *Port Fairy*, that evening was Oberleutnant Joachim Ohm, the Operations Officer of III./KG 40. It was hit on the port quarter by a 50 kg bomb that breached the hull, set the ship on fire and disabled its steering. Ammunition was jettisoned and compartments flooded to lessen the risk of explosion, and attempts were made to douse the fire, assisted by HMS *Swale*'s fire hoses. By 0041 hrs on 13 July the fires were under control, and the *Port Fairy* limped 500 nautical miles to Casablanca – none of its crew was injured or killed.

Survivors from the *Duchess of York* and *California* were picked up by their escorts and also taken to Casablanca. The burning hulks of both liners were then sunk by their escorts so as not to present a beacon to German submarines and aircraft. The convoy 'Faith' disaster was both a shock and an embarrassment to the Allies, as the Luftwaffe had rarely managed to carry out successful attacks on troopships in the past. The loss of these vessels and personnel destined for Africa, the Middle and Far East had taught the Allies a painful, but valuable, lesson. From now on, convoys would sail further to the west, out of range of Condors but bringing them closer to the U-boats, which could in turn be handled by the escorts.

Despite the spectacularly successful attack on convoy 'Faith', Condor crews were finding it increasingly difficult to sink enemy ships. As with previous months, July 1943 also saw KG 40 suffer at the hands of marauding Allied fighters ranging further afield in search of Fw 200s. Two were duly shot down by Beaufighters of No 248 Sqn, the first on the 9th and the second on the 29th. Unteroffizier Rudolf Schöwe of 2./KG 40 was part of the Condor crew shot down on the latter date;

'In December 1941 we were retrained on the Fw 200. At the beginning of 1942 we were transferred to Trondheim for a year. From there we initially attacked convoys sailing from Reykjavik to Murmansk and Archangelsk. Later we carried out attacks on single ships.

'In January 1943 we took part in resupplying the 6th Army, which had been encircled in Stalingrad, using different Russian airfields. Afterwards we operated against convoys. Flying from Bordeaux-Mérignac, we took off for our last flight on 29 July 1943. We met a large convoy sailing from Tangier to England [SL 133] and successfully, as we thought, bombed a freighter from an altitude of 3000 m [9800 ft]. Because of the heavy flak from the escorting warships we did not have time to see the results of our attack.

'On our return flight we were attacked by two twin-engined aircraft and shot down about 300 miles west of Cape Finisterre. In the course of these attacks our first pilot, Oberfeldwebel Alfred Bolfrass, was killed, but the second pilot, Unteroffizier Gnuechtel, was able to ditch the burning plane. Wearing our lifejackets, the rest of the crew, some wounded, left the aircraft for the dinghy. The next day we heard the loud noise of battle and later we learned that three U-boats [U-461, U-462 and U-504] had been sunk near to where we had been shot down.

'Early in the morning of 31 July, at about 0200 hrs, we were fished out by a British warship that had been involved in this battle.'

The composite report of this action submitted by No 248 Sqn perfectly matches Schöwe's account;

'Beaufighters of No 248 Sqn were at 100 ft when they sighted a Fw 200 one mile distant ahead flying at 100 ft. Aircraft A, who made the first sighting, immediately turned, followed by U, J and S, and fired a long burst of cannon fire from 300 yards range. Attacking from enemy's port quarter, hits were scored on port wing root and cockpit. Beaufighter A now found himself astern of enemy aircraft and fired another long burst of cannon fire from 150 yards. Following this attack both port engines caught fire.

Fw 200C-4 Wk-Nr 0132 F8+CK of 2./KG 40 was shot down by Beaufighters from No 248 Sqn 300 miles west of Cape Finisterre on 29 July 1943. The surviving crewmen (the co-pilot had been killed in the attack) were rescued by a British warship two days later

Fw 200C-4 Wk-Nr 0095 F8+CD of *Stab* III./KG 40 was routinely flown by Oberleutnant Joachim Ohm, who damaged the *Port Fairy* during the convoy 'Faith' attack. Photographed from the Condor flown by Oberleutnant Herbert Fobker, this aircraft had been lost six months prior to the 'Faith' mission. Assigned to KGzbV 200, it was written off on 19 January 1943 during the Stalingrad airlift

'Aircraft A then broke away to port and Beaufighter U came in to attack from enemy's port quarter, firing a short burst followed by a long burst of cannon fire. No results could be seen from this attack as port engines were giving off much smoke, but pilot is confident that hits were scored. Aircraft U then broke away to port and aircraft S came in to attack. Enemy aircraft was now gliding gently downwards and S fired a long burst from starboard quarter. Hits were scored on starboard inner engine.

'Fw 200 was now skimming along the wave tops and ditched shortly afterwards. Eight of the crew were seen swimming in the water. The fire had apparently been extinguished and the enemy aircraft was left floating when the Beaufighters left.'

Credit for this kill was shared between Plt Off P A S Payne (Beaufighter A), Lt 'Gaston Newman' (alias Claude Serf in Beaufighter S) and Flg Offs Fred Lacy (Beaufighter J) and J K Thompson (Beaufighter U).

Long-ranging USAAF units were now also inflicting losses on the Condor force, including B-24 Liberator-equipped 480th Anti-Submarine Group (ASG). It was destined to have five noteworthy combats with Fw 200s of KG 40. On 28 July 1Lt Elbert Hyde and his crew shot down the aeroplane flown by Oberfeldwebel Rudolf Waschek from 2./KG 40. Three days later it was the turn of Capt Gerald Mosier and his crew, who shot down Oberleutnant Siegfried Gall's Condor from 7./KG 40. On this occasion the B-24 crew was on an anti-submarine sweep when, flying in heavy cloud, the search radar in their Liberator detected an aeroplane seven miles ahead. Mosier altered course towards it, and when the contact was about a mile away he descended through cloud. The ensuing action, described in a journal at the time, again shows how these running battles between Condors and various Allied aircraft were fought;

'There it was, dead ahead about 500 ft below them and 1500 yards out – a big Fw 200 Condor. This was their first combat, the time when all their training had to take hold. The top turret swung around, the bombardier manned the 0.50-calibre in the nose and the pilot hit the throttle and closed in to 600 yards. It was apparent the Fw 200 was being taken by surprise, as it took no evasive action. The upper turret opened fire with twin 0.50-calibre and moments later the bombardier began firing his single machine gun from the nose. The first bursts from these guns overshot the Condor, but the alarm was given and the giant plane began taking evasive action. Its pilot dropped 500 ft and turned sharply left. Then the top turret gunner in the Condor began firing back, but his aim was wide and to the right. As it did, the right waist gunner got a look at the Liberator and opened fire but his deflection was way off too.

'Now the Condor did a diving corkscrew turn to almost 500 ft above the Atlantic. Again, the Liberator followed and its upper turret got a clean shot. Twin streams of bullets arched out and struck home on the Condor. They ate into the port inner engine and across the fuselage into the starboard inner engine before the Condor jerked desperately away.

'It was that moment that the Condor's ventral gunner had been waiting for. The Liberator came into his sights and he sent a stream of 20 mm shells back and down. They hit home on the leading edge of the port wing just inboard of the No 2 engine, ate back along the fuselage and into the top of the starboard rudder. Then the Liberator was gone from his sights as the pilot climbed with full throttle to again get above the Condor.'

For 11 minutes both aircraft shot at each other. In the Liberator, the top turret was now out of ammunition and it looked as if there would be no clear winner. However, it appears that Oberleutnant Gall decided to break off and make for France, which gave the Liberator one final chance;

'The bombardier squeezed his trigger. His last bullets spat out in a stream. They hit the Condor's wing root and centre fuselage and suddenly an intense fire broke out and smoke came pouring back. The Liberator pulled up as the bombardier's gun stopped firing. For a moment, the giant plane wavered as if the pilot had lost control, then he steadied it. All four engines were still operating at full throttle as he fought to hold it, racing along just above the Atlantic and gushing smoke and fire. Then, without warning, the Condor's port wing struck the water. It ricocheted off and the plane shot forward for another 300 yards before its nose dropped and it plunged into the sea and exploded with a great geyser of smoke, ocean and flame.'

Although one crewman was seen to bail out, the last that the Germans heard from Gall's crew was that they were involved in a dogfight at 1242 hrs. Not surprisingly, there were no survivors. Mosier received the DFC for this combat.

Aside from the aeroplanes lost in combat, KG 40 had also experienced a handful of accidents in July. A number of Fw 200s had been damaged and two written off. In personnel terms, 17 crewmen had lost their lives, 11 had been captured and four injured.

Attrition continued into August, with the first combat casualty of the month, on the 5th, turning out to be the USAAF's only Arctic Circle aerial victory claim of the war. It also heralded the last combat loss for KG 40 in Icelandic waters. As a result of increased German air activity the year before, the USAAF decided to strengthen Iceland's fighter defences. The 50th FS replaced the 27th FS in August 1942, and it remained here until February 1944. Actions were few and far between after that, however, with just one kill – a Ju 88D-5 of 1(F)/120 – occurring on 24 April 1943. The next, and last, combat occurred on 5 August 1943.

At 0800 hrs that day Oberfeldwebel Karl Holtrup of 3./KG 40 took off from Trondheim-Værnes to carry out a reconnaissance mission between Iceland and Greenland. After five hours all that the German crew had seen was a lone fishing boat, which they circled, photographed and then turned back on course. Then they spotted something in the distance and turned to investigate. This was a fatal mistake, as shortly afterwards two P-38 Lightnings were seen in the glare of the sun, headed towards them. Lts Dick Holly and Bill Bethea had been detached to Kassos Field with orders to protect the Icelandic herring fleet from German aircraft. Holly described what happened next;

'I had been sent to this small airstrip on the north coast because it had been reported that German planes had been coming over from Norway and had been harassing the Icelandic fishing fleet. After a few days of patrolling, my wingman, Lt Bill Bethea, and I encountered a big German plane and I immediately opened fire, setting ablaze the port wing. The German pilot did an outstanding job of ditching the plane and the entire crew got into a dinghy, and the plane sank within minutes.

'I sent Bill back to our field to refuel while I kept the dinghy in view and contacted the US Navy, who had an outpost nearby. I don't remember how long it took, but they did get out to pick up the entire crew, who were uninjured except for a foot wound to one crew member.'

Holly's rounds had hit the port fuel tank, which then caught fire and burned through the hydraulic lines, causing the port undercarriage to drop down. Both port engines then started to lose power and, with the fire spreading, the flight engineer urged that they ditch or face being blown apart when the remaining fuel exploded. Wisely, Holtrup ditched immediately north of Grimsey.

Further south, the 480th ASG made its presence felt once again eight days later when 1Lt Fred McKinnon and his crew had a running battle with Oberleutnant Günther Seide at altitudes ranging from 2000 ft down to sea level. The B-24's gunners expended no fewer than 1790 rounds of 0.50-calibre ammunition. The Condor's gunners failed to hit the B-24, and eventually the Fw 200's No 3 engine started to smoke and the aircraft subsequently crash-landed in Spain. McKinnon received the DFC for the action. Unteroffizier Werner Zerrahn of 9./KG 40 recalled what happened;

'13 August 1943. In almost all cases we had been briefed to fly an armed reconnaissance sortie over the Bay of Biscay as far as to the Azores. Flights like this had a duration of about 10-12 hours and our aircraft carried four 250 kg bombs and later two Henschel Hs 293A radio-controlled missiles.

An aerial view of Oberleutnant Günther Seide's Fw 200C-5/U1 Wk-Nr 0221 after it had force-landed in a harvested field of maize at Camarinas, in Spain, on 13 August 1943. The aeroplane had been undertaking an armed reconnaissance sortie over the Bay of Biscay as far west as the Azores when it became involved in a running battle with a B-24 Liberator of the 480th ASG

'During our approach we were able to make out a convoy, and reported its position to Bordeaux-Mérignac by sending a coded radio message. Only a few minutes later a B-24 Liberator appeared which caused us a lot of trouble. The enemy's speed was considerably higher than ours and we received many hits. Our gunner, Obergefreiter Heinz Wagner, was wounded and holes in the fuel tanks caused the loss of quite an amount of fuel. Fortunately, we reached a layer of cloud, and with the last drop of fuel we were able to make a good belly-landing in a harvested field of maize near La Coruna, in Spain. After spending a few days in La Coruna and Valladolid we came to Madrid, and two weeks later we arrived back at Bordeaux.'

Despite recent losses, III./KG 40 despatched no fewer than 21 Condors, led by Major Robert Kowalewski (who had recently taken command of KG 40 and would hand over III./KG 40 to Hauptmann Walter Rieder), on 15 August to attack convoy OS 53/ KMS 23 220 miles northwest of Lisbon. They were credited with sinking the 6060 GRT steamer *Warfield* (94 crew were rescued and two killed) and damaging two others, although Oberleutnant Bernhard Kunisch's Fw 200C-4 from 7./KG 40 was apparently damaged by HMS *Stork* and had to force-land at Lavacolla, near Santander in Spain. He and his crew returned, only for them to be shot down and killed on 20 November 1943. Such an effort could not be repeated, as losses and unserviceability were bleeding KG 40 dry, especially as the Condors were still trying to remain as effective as possible from as far north as Iceland down to the Azores.

On 17 August the 480th ASG's Capt Hugh Maxwell Jr and his crew shot down the Fw 200 flown by Oberfeldwebel Karl Bauer of 2./KG 40. They also apparently damaged the Condor from the same *Staffel* flown by Oberleutnant Heinz Küchenmeister. The latter was reported to have crash-landed back at Bordeaux-Mérignac, although subsequent research seems to disprove this. Maxwell Jr's B-24 was damaged in this action too, however, and three crew were lost when the aeroplane ditched shortly thereafter. Following the very last combat between the 480th ASG and an unidentified Fw 200, on 28 August, 1Lt Fred McKinnon (who had shot down Oberleutnant Günther Seide four days earlier) force-landed at Langosteira, in Spain.

Six Fw 200s had been lost in combat (two aeroplanes landing in Spain) and one ditched as result of an accident during August, resulting in 11 aircrew being killed, 11 captured and one injured. The next two months saw a decrease in Condor losses, with two aircraft being shot down in September and three written off in accidents in October. Coastal Command reported seeing just two Fw 200s during this period. However, changes were afoot.

At the end of November the remainder of I./KG 40 moved from Trondheim-Værnes to Fassberg to start converting to the He 177 – the Heinkel had flown its first operational missions over the Mediterranean with II./KG 40 on 21 November 1943. However, the *Gruppe's* Condor-equipped 3. *Staffel*, commanded by Hauptmann Robert Maly, remained at Trondheim-Værnes. Furthermore, in a confusing series of moves, 2./KG 40, led by Hauptmann Kurt Herzog, became subordinate to III./KG 40, now

Victors and vanquished from the action on 5 August 1943 come together at Patterson Field, on Iceland, nine days later. These men are, from left to right, Oberfeldwebel Emil Brand and Karl Holtrup, Lt Bill Bethea (of the 50th FS), Feldwebel Josef Teufel, Gefreiter Wilhelm Lehn, Lt Dick Holly (also from the 50th FS), Obergefreiter Siegfried Klinkmann and Unteroffizier Herbert Richter (with his ankle in plaster) and Günter Karte. Bethea and Holly had downed the 3./KG 40 Fw 200, flown by Oberfeldwebel Karl Holtrup, during its reconnaissance mission from Trondheim-Værnes to the waters between Iceland and Greenland

commanded by Hauptmann Walter Rieder. On 24 November, 2. and 8./KG 40 (the latter unit flying He 177s under the leadership of Major Fritz Hoppe) swapped designations, with 8. *Staffel* becoming 2./KG 40 in an all-He 177 *Gruppe* and 2. *Staffel* becoming 8./KG 40 in an all-Fw 200 *Gruppe*. The remaining Condor *Staffelkapitäns* were Oberleutnant Joachim Ohm (7./KG 40) and Hauptmann Wilhelm Dette (9./KG 40). The Condor's future was clearly limited, as KG 40 now had I. and II. *Gruppe* equipped with the He 177 and only III./KG 40 flying the Fw 200.

Other changes were also afoot. By the summer of 1943 the Luftwaffe had two air-launched guided weapons for anti-shipping operations. The first was the Ruhrstahl FX 1400, or 'Fritz X', stand-off bomb, which carried a 3300-lb warhead. 'Fritz X' was released from altitudes between 16,000 ft and 20,000 ft and, falling at near terminal velocity, was guided by a bomb aimer who was aided by a flare in the weapon's tail. The second weapon was the Henschel Hs 293, which carried an 1100-lb warhead. A small rocket motor accelerated the missile to about 370 mph and cut out after 12 seconds, whereupon the bomb coasted to its target in a shallow glide, again guided by a bomb aimer who was aided by a small flare in the bomb's tail. The latter weapon was launched from the Condor, and several Fw 200C-3s and C-4s were converted to carry an Hs 293 beneath each wing, outboard of the outer engine nacelles. Such aircraft were designated Fw 200C-6s, but the Fw 200C-8 was designed specifically as a launch platform for the Hs 293. The weapon made its combat debut with the Condor on 28 December 1943.

The previous month had brought yet more losses for the Fw 200. On 14 November Oberfeldwebel Richard Liebe of 3./KG 40 crashed his Condor into the sea 80 km northwest of Eidsa during a convoy reconnaissance mission, and Oberleutnant Herbert Leuschner of 9./KG 40 went down near Stuttgart during a ferry flight on the 26th, killing the crew of six and five passengers. Just how difficult it was becoming for Condor crews (and how easy a target the aeroplane was for Allied fighter pilots) is best related by Flt Sgt Charlie Tomalin of No 248 Sqn, who was involved in a Fw 200 interception on 20 November;

'Four Beaufighters in loose formation flying westerly at about 1000 ft. I was on the port side nearest the Spanish coast when I spotted an Fw 200 on my port side at nine o'clock flying east. I broke radio silence to inform Flg Off Green, but he did not reply immediately so I decided to attack as I was in the best position. I selected all guns to fire and camera on, did a steep turn to port, got the Fw 200 in my gunsight, allowed for deflection and gravity and fired about a five-second burst. I completed a circle at zero feet and saw that the starboard outer engine was aflame and it was just about to ditch. I was momentarily mesmerised by my first-ever attack against an aircraft, but soon recovered when a line of splashes showed in the sea – a gunner on the stricken Fw 200 was still aiming at my Beau when perhaps he should have been at crash station. I admired his pluck!'

Oberleutnant Bernhard Kunisch and his crew of six, including Hauptmann Horst Lückstadt, were all reported missing.

If November had been a bad month for III./KG 40, December proved to be even worse. The *Gruppe*'s first loss came on the first day of the month, as Lt Dick Fleischmann-Allen of 842 NAS (equipped with Martlet IVs) explained;

Fw 200C-6 Wk-Nr 0218 F8+AD of *Stab* III./KG 40, flown by Oberleutnant Alfred Arzinger, heads for convoy OS 53/KMS 53 off the Portuguese coast on the afternoon of 15 August 1943. This aircraft would crash near Drontheim on 14 August 1944 during a crew training flight, killing Oberleutnant Rudolf Biberger (*Gruppenadjutant*) and five crewmen – there was one survivor

'Lt Les Wort and I were vectored on to the target immediately after takeoff from HMS *Fencer* in order to effect a rapid interception at a sufficient altitude to obtain a height advantage. It was apparent that the crew of the Fw 200 were completely oblivious to our proximity until such time as we actually commenced our attack runs. Return fire was sporadic and ineffective (although my aircraft did receive a hit in the oil cooler, fortunately with no dire consequences). Likewise, avoiding action by the Condor pilot was almost non-existent.

'When we had completed our runs there was obviously substantial power failure, as the enemy lost height immediately once we had broken away. As I recollect, there was no sign of damage, but I remember the aircraft smoking once it was on the water. It had made a pancake landing, allowing some of the crew to escape into their dinghy – the sea was reasonably calm and when we left the scene after circling the wreckage, the aircraft was still afloat and the crew were waving to us. I have often wondered if any of them survived – I would doubt it, as the action took place a long way from land.'

There were no survivors from Oberleutnant Joachim Knauthe's crew from 8./KG 40, with all eight airmen still reported as missing.

Eleven days later Oberfeldwebel Kurt Metzmann of 8./KG 40 hit a power cable during a training flight, his Condor crashing at St Sulpice, near Limoges in France. Seven crew were killed and one injured. On the 13th the first Fw 200C-6 was lost in action, as recalled by one of its radio operators, Feldwebel Hans Rassek of 7./KG 40;

This unusual photograph, taken from the cockpit of Oberleutnant Joachim Ohm's F8+CD, shows Major Robert Kowalewski's F8+AA in the lead during the large-scale raid mounted by III./KG 40 on convoy OS 53/KMS 23 when it was 220 miles northwest of Lisbon on 15 August 1943. No fewer than 21 Condors were despatched from Bordeaux-Mérignac, and they were credited with sinking the 6060 GRT steamer *Warfield* and damaging two others during this attack

The charred remains of Fw 200C-6 Wk-Nr 0237 F8+MR of 7./KG 40 at Dromineer, in County Tipperary, following its forced landing by Unteroffizier Hans Meidel on 13 December 1943. The aeroplane had had two engines knocked out by AA fire during an attack on convoy ON 214, leaving the crew with little choice but to crash-land in Ireland. They blew the Condor up prior to being interned by the Irish authorities (*via Irish Air Corps*)

This recently delivered Fw 200C-8 was photographed at Bordeaux-Mérignac in the summer of 1943. The aeroplane, which appears to be unarmed, has had antennae for the FuG 200 Hohentweil search radar fitted to its nose and a Lotfe 7D bombsight mounted at the front of the ventral gondola. The FuG 200 was used in conjunction with a blind bombing procedure and was accurate to a range of less than a mile. The final version of the Condor to enter production, only nine C-8s had been built when construction of the Fw 200 came to an end in February 1944. A further 17 older C-models were also upgraded to C-8 standard

'13 December – We had been briefed to locate a convoy [ON 214] in the area south of Iceland. With this aim, we flew from Cognac to Lorient first. There, we refuelled, as we expected a long flight time. Late in the afternoon we found the convoy but, we were hit by flak. Two engines broke down and we had no choice but to change course and head for the nearest land. After we were sure we would not come down in Northern Ireland, we decided to carry out an emergency landing in the Republic of Ireland. Very quickly we decided not to bail out because it was so dark, but on seeing the bright lights of Nenagh, in Tipperary, it seemed to be the right place for an emergency landing, especially as there was a hospital there.

'We were lucky. Unteroffizier Hans Meidel's masterly flying performance (with his strong nerves, he was the one that brought us down) meant that we landed with no serious consequences. We then blew the aircraft up and were interned.'

There was now a lull in the action until 21 December, when *Befehlshaber der U-Boot* and *Marinegruppe West* requested maximum reconnaissance sorties from this date onwards in support of the German blockade runners *Alsterufer* and *Osorno* returning to the Bay of Biscay – an event that had not been missed by either the Royal Navy or Coastal Command. His Majesty's Ships *Enterprise*, *Glasgow*, *Gambia*, *Penelope* and *Ariadne*, together with the French warships *Le Fantasque* and *Le Malin*, were all involved in hunting down these vessels. The *Alsterufer* was in fact crippled by a Liberator from No 311 Sqn during the afternoon of 27 December and later abandoned. The following day, warships of 8. *Zerstörer Flottille* and 4. *Torpedo Flottille*, which had been sent into the Bay to escort both blockade breakers, were intercepted first by American Consolidated PB5Y-1s of Fleet Air Wing 7 and then by *Glasgow* and *Enterprise*, which

Seen while testing the Hs 293 at Karlshagen in early 1943, Fw 200C-5FK Wk-Nr 0226 DP+ON has a single guided bomb mounted on each underwing stores rack

resulted in the sinking of Z27, T25 and T26 and the loss of more than 400 German sailors.

Supporting this operation put extra pressure on III./KG 40's groundcrew to have the maximum number of aircraft mission ready. So it was that at 0630 hrs on 28 December, four Fw 200s managed to get airborne from Cognac. One of the Condors was captained by 33-year-old Hauptmann Wilhelm Dette, *Staffelkapitän* of 9./KG 40, who was forced to fly a 7./KG 40 aircraft owing to unserviceability. A highly experienced Condor pilot, Dette had been awarded the *Ehrenpokal* in December 1941 and the *Deutsches Kreuz in Gold* in April 1942 while with 1./KG 40. His Condor was the only one of the four carrying Hs 293s. If any Allied warship was spotted, Dette intended to approach using cloud cover, carrying out a surprise attack, and then use the same cloud cover to get away. Flight engineer Unteroffizier Willi Hackler recalled what happened during the mission;

'At the end of October through to the beginning of November our crew was in Peenemünde to receive training on how to drop glide bombs. On 28 December we took off from Cognac at 0600 hrs. I do not know what kind of patrol pattern we were flying, "Streifenaufklärung" (strip reconnaissance) or "Fächeraufklärung" (fanwise reconnaissance).'

At 1040 hrs a Sunderland was spotted, both aircraft emerging from cloud simultaneously. Hackler fired a quick burst before both aeroplanes again disappeared into cloud. The presence of the Condor was not noted by the Sunderland crew. Hackler continued;

'The contact with the Sunderland was in no way a real dogfight. I was sitting at my 13 mm MG 131 machine gun in the aft dorsal position. Looking from my position, the Sunderland appeared out of the clouds above and to the right, at a distance of about 150 metres [160 yards]. The enemy plane immediately turned to the left and climbed into the clouds, presenting its underside. I fired two short bursts with my machine gun. It is unlikely that the Sunderland had shot at us because, as far as I know, there was no ventral gun position. I cannot say for sure if we were already on our return flight.

'The outer starboard engine showed a small trail of white smoke or even petrol. Via intercom I reported, "Herr Hauptmann, we must not turn off the engine otherwise there will be a fire on board!" Flames came out of the exhaust pipes when you cut the engines. I did not get a reply. After about ten minutes had passed, Oberfeldwebel Günther turned off the engine and, as I had predicted, it burst into flames. Then Hauptmann Dette gave the order to put on our parachutes, but nobody did. Smoke came into the fuselage. Oberfeldwebel Sewing was the first into the back part of the fuselage, where I was. Both of us pushed the inflatable dinghy to the door. I pulled the emergency lever and kicked out the door. In the meantime Unteroffiziers Lelewel and Schmidt had also arrived in this part of the aircraft. We came closer and closer to the water, the engines did not roar any more and then there was a terrible rattling noise.

'Water is much more solid than it looks, and the plane came to a standstill very fast. The starboard engine was torn out of the wing and had flown through the air. When I regained my consciousness again water was washing around me. One of the big tanks was lying directly on me, but I managed to crawl to the door, open the air bottle of my lifejacket and then jump into the water. My comrades and the rubber dinghy were about 15 metres [50 ft] away from me. When I arrived at the dinghy I noticed that my lifejacket had been damaged, and so I was more a non-swimmer than a swimmer. It took about 30 minutes to make our four-man dinghy seaworthy. Oberfeldwebel Sewing was drifting in the sea some distance from our dinghy, and he called, "Help me, I want to get back to my little boy!" Terrible!

'I think I do not have to describe the conditions in a four-man dinghy occupied by six men. During the second night we heard the noise of an engine above and fired a signal flare. The aircraft dropped floating lights and circled for about 30 minutes. Next morning, at about 1000 hrs, we saw a small dot far away on the horizon. We thought it was an aeroplane, so we set fire to the signal flare, which was part of the dinghy's equipment. This caused a huge cloud of red smoke. We were discovered by an American aircraft. After flying a few circles the aeroplane dropped some parcels, watertight but easy to open by hand. They contained highly nutritious food and water. But the food was too sweet, which meant we got very

Newly built Fw 200C-8 TO+XO clearly shows the nose-mounted antennae associated with the FuG 200 Hohentweil search radar

thirsty from it and there was only half a bottle of water per parcel.

'The aircraft kept contact for about four hours. Another aeroplane arrived at night and again during the day until, at about 2300 hrs on the fourth night, we could see searchlights far away on the horizon. More than once we fired recognition signals, and on 1 January 1944, at about 0200 hrs, the ship eventually arrived.'

Dette had ditched with the Hs 293s attached, which broke the force of the impact and helped keep the Condor afloat long enough for the crew to get into a dinghy. The six survivors were rescued by the ASW trawler HMS *Lord Nuffield*.

One more Condor was lost before the year was out, Oberfeldwebel Wilhelm Friedrich's Fw 200C-8 from 7./KG 40 failing to return from a sortie over the Bay of Biscay on 30 December. His crew of seven included yet another experienced officer, 33-year-old Hauptmann Georg Schobert, who had flown as an observer in a number of units from the start of the war, including KG 51 and I./KG 50.

Hauptmann Georg Schobert (standing fourth from left) poses with his crew in the autumn of 1943. On 30 December 1943 he was part of Oberfeldwebel Wilhelm Friedrich's seven-man crew that failed to return from a sortie over the Bay of Biscay in an Fw 200C-8 from 7./KG 40

If that was not bad enough, on 31 December USAAF heavy bombers targeted Bordeaux-Mérignac, Cognac and Landes airfields. Oberleutnant Herbert Fobker of 9./KG 40 had had to abort a mission early because of engine problems, and Cognac was attacked shortly after he had landed. He and his crew hurried into slit trenches, but the one that Fobker and Leutnant Rudolf Hieber were in suffered a direct hit and both men were killed. Although just 21 years old, Fobker had flown operationally with 8. and 9./KG 40 from the end of May 1941, first in He 111s and then Fw 200s. He had been shot down into the North Sea by Spitfires of No 266 Sqn on 19 August 1941, Fobker and his crew being rescued 116 hours later. He had been awarded the *Frontflugspange in Gold* on 10 December 1942, the *Ehrenpokal* on 15 March 1943 and the *Deutsches Kreuz in Gold* on 17 October 1943.

On 31 December almost 300 B-17s from the Eighth Air Force's 1st, 2nd and 3rd Bomb Divisions targeted Bordeaux-Mérignac, Cognac and Landes airfields, destroying a number of Fw 200s and severely damaging base infrastructure. This aircraft suffered a direct hit during the raid on Cognac

In the space of just four days three highly experienced officers from III./KG 40 had been killed, and in the last two months of the year eight Condors had been lost, with 45 aircrew killed, eight interned and six made PoWs. These losses, with little chance of replacement, raised serious questions about the viability of the Fw 200. Events early in the new year would quickly show that the Condor had a very limited future.

CHAPTER FIVE

1944 – NOWHERE TO HIDE

The remains of Fw 200C-4 Wk-Nr 0170 at Saint Juest on 5 February 1944, this aircraft having been shot down by P-38s from the 20th FG shortly after it attempted to flee a strafing attack on Avord airfield. Of the ten men on board the Condor only five survived.

January 1944 started badly, with another attack on Bordeaux-Mérignac resulting in the destruction of some eight Condors and the damaging of three more. The first operational loss was the Fw 200C-5 commanded by Oberleutnant Ernst Rebensburg, which failed to return from a mission between Norway and Iceland on 17 January. Rebensburg and his crew of six were still flying as part of 3./KG 40, although the *Staffel* was on the strength of III./KG 40, as 1. and 2./KG 40 were now flying the He 177.

More and more German aircraft, including Condors, now began to fall prey to RAF and USAAF long-range fighters over land, rather than over the sea. The first loss to an Allied intruder had probably taken place as early as 31 July 1942, when the Fw 200C-3 of IV./KG 40's Oberleutnant Hermann Frenzel crash-landed and burnt out after being attacked during a nocturnal training flight by a Mosquito of No 23 Sqn. The crew of the latter aircraft, Wg Cdr Bertie Hoare and Plt Off Sydney Cornes, claimed an unidentified aircraft near Orleans. Frenzel and a second crewman were wounded during the attack. It was not until the first month of 1944 that the next loss to an intruder occurred. On 27 January Flt Lt Charles Scherf and Flg Off Al Brown, in a Mosquito of No 418 Sqn, shot down a Condor of 9./KG 40 near Avord, in France, killing Oberfeldwebel Willi Schmidt and four crew;

'An Fw 200 was seen 120 miles ahead, southeast of Avord going west. Flt Lt Scherf turned sharply to starboard and attacked from astern, range 500 yards and height 300 ft. Seven- to eight-second burst, strikes on port wing moving forward to fuselage – under part of fuselage caught fire. Wg Cdr D C S Macdonald took cine camera shots. Pieces flew off and enemy aircraft levelled out. As pilot was bailing out, Wg Cdr Macdonald fired at enemy aircraft and engine burst into flames. Enemy aircraft crashed in a wood at 1630 hrs.'

Two days later, four Hawker Typhoons of No 247 Sqn, led by Wg Cdr Erik Haabjoern, shot down a Condor of 12./KG 40 south of Chateaudun, in France, resulting in the deaths of Feldwebel Karl Miklas, three of his crew and a handful of passengers. Condors simply did not survive against such modern, heavily armed, combat aircraft.

There was another loss to an intruder on 5 February, when the aircraft in which Obergefreiter Artur Steig was a passenger was destroyed. Four months earlier, Steig, an aircraft ground engineer, had been sent to Peenemünde to train on glide bombs. He then joined III./KG 40 at Avord on 4 February 1944. The day after his arrival Steig was told that III./KG 40 would be attacking a convoy in the Mediterranean, and that they had to fly to Cognac first to load up with the Hs 293s. Steig's Fw 200C-4, flown by Hauptmann Ingeniur Anton Leder, took off as planned but had to turn back due to adverse weather. However, as they were taxiing back in, Avord came under attack by B-17s of the USAAF's 1st Bomb Division. Steig recalls what happened next;

'To prevent our Condors from being destroyed, we were ordered to take off immediately. That meant aircraft took off in all directions, and to avoid a collision, our plane had to turn and begin a new takeoff run. We were lucky, as we were not hit by bombs, but now our aeroplane was completely alone in the sky.'

A total of 210 Republic P-47 Thunderbolts, P-38s and North American P-51s provided escorts for attacks by 547 B-17s on five different airfields that day. One of the escorting units was the 20th FG, flying P-38s from Kingscliffe, in Northamptonshire. The group took off at 0912 hrs, rendezvoused with two combat wings of B-17s south of Le Havre and escorted them to their target at Orleans. However, as they approached Avord, the USAAF pilots spotted 12 'large aircraft' preparing to take off. After four had managed to get airborne, Group CO Col Barton Russell ordered the 77th FS, commanded by Lt Col Robert Montgomery, to attack, leaving the 55th FS to provide top cover and the 79th FS to remain with the bombers.

Lt Jack Davies, part of White Section, was acting as wingman to White Leader, Capt Paul Sabo. Davies subsequently recalled;

'We spotted an Fw 200 flying down on the deck at about 1000 ft altitude and headed south. We attacked at once, descending in a 270-degree right turn down to 500 ft, and attacked from the left-hand side. The left waist gunner was clearly visible and firing at us as we approached. Sabo and I, firing simultaneously, must have hit the Fw 200's fuel tanks or some other explosive material, resulting in a major explosion. We went up and over the Fw 200 in a climbing turn and saw it crash on fire into the ground. I said to myself if anyone escaped that crash it would be a miracle.'

Steig recalled the one-sided engagement from his perspective;

'Our Fw 200 had been refuelled with 6000 litres, and because of the attack the fuel tanks burst into flames. Our pilot and one of the gunners were killed instantly, and because we mechanics had not been given parachutes the second pilot, Unteroffizier Kurt Frosch, announced that he had decided to try an emergency landing. I think it was more of a crash than an emergency landing, and when I regained consciousness the whole aeroplane was on fire, as were my clothes. The fuselage had rolled over several times, so the machine gun mountings had been ripped out, which made it possible for me to climb out. Two of my comrades were then killed by exploding ammunition after they had left the aircraft.'

The crash occurred at Saint Juest, six miles southwest of Avord. Four crew were killed and three injured, plus one of the groundcrew perished and two were injured, including Steig. The burns to his hands were so serious that he was hospitalised, initially at Saint Dieux and then Orleans, until the end of June 1944.

The first combat loss over the Bay of Biscay occurred on 12 February when up to six Condors took off to attack convoy OS 67/KMS 41, which was about 400 miles west of Cape Finisterre. The *Stab* III./KG 40 aircraft flown by Oberleutnant Günther Seide and his crew included Unteroffizier Werner Zerrahn, who had been in an Fw 200 that had force-landed in Spain on 13 August 1943. This time the Seide crew would again be lucky, as Zerrahn recalled;

'We had taken off with about five or six aircraft, and on our way out we spotted some twin-engined aeroplanes to starboard ahead, and assumed it would be our own escort of Ju 88s from I./ZG 1. However, these aeroplanes now took an attacking position by flying a steep turn, and we realised they were enemy aircraft. As far as I remember we were attacked only once – we escaped with minor damage. I suffered a bullet graze to my left foot and Feldwebel Günther Hickmann, a radio operator in another aircraft, was shot through the left hand. Back on the ground we found out that we had had a lot of luck because we counted 130 bullet holes in our Condor.'

They had indeed been lucky, the Fw 200 being intercepted by three Mosquitoes of No 157 Sqn on an 'Instep' patrol. Feldwebel Karl-Heinz Schairer of 7./KG 40 was not so fortunate as his aircraft was downed by Flt Lts Dick 'Dolly' Doleman and Brian Whitlock and Flg Off Verdun Hannawin. Schairer and his seven crewmen were all reported missing. In Seide's aircraft, Werner Zerrahn had probably been wounded by Verdun Hannawin. The combat report from this mission shows just how one-sided the combat on 12 February was;

'Flt Lt Doleman sighted aircraft on the starboard beam about four miles away and the three Mosquitoes turned starboard towards them. The aircraft were seen to be five Fw 200s, four in V formation and one straggling, flying at 0 feet – our aircraft attacked from starboard in line astern, each opening fire at about 900 yards, closing to 600 yards. Strikes were scored on at least one enemy aircraft, the last on the starboard side of the V. Flt Lt Doleman broke away to port, the other two to starboard.

'Flt Lt Doleman and Flg Off Hannawin re-formed and attacked again from the starboard quarter. As Flt Lt Doleman attacked, the inner starboard engine of the enemy aircraft damaged in the first attack caught fire, and fire also broke out on the starboard side of the fuselage. When Flg Off Hannawin attacked, the flames spread all over the wing, the enemy aircraft doing a gentle turn to starboard, losing height, hitting the sea and immediately blowing up. During the course of this attack Flg Off Hannawin also scored strikes on the other aircraft on the starboard side of the enemy formation. Flg Off Hannawin made two more attacks on the remaining four aircraft before setting course for base.'

Zerrahn's luck held. After this, III./KG 40 moved to Trondheim, but owing to a lack of aircraft, fuel and crews, he was transferred to the Wehrmacht's 6. *Fallschirmjäger*-Division and took part in the Battle of the Bulge. He was captured by American troops near Prüm on 31 January 1945. However. Zerrahn's pilot, Günther Seide, was killed on a ferry flight from Gotenhafen to Schwerin on 11 May 1944 when his Fw 200C-5 suffered a double engine failure and crashed at Kunersdorf.

Encounters at sea were now becoming rare, with Coastal Command recording just three engagements with Condors during 1944 – on 26 and 30 May off the Shetlands and on 8 June over the Bay of Biscay. All three were uneventful. Meanwhile, intruder attacks continued to cause losses in Condors and personnel, with both air- and groundcrew being casualties. For example, on 5 March the 4th and 357th FGs optimistically claimed seven Condors at Bergerac, Bordeaux-Mérignac and Parthenay during low-level attacks on airfields in the area. Surviving German records confirm that a number of Fw 200s were indeed scrambled from St Jean D'Angely, with Feldwebel Hermann Wesemann of 7./KG 40 successfully crash-landing just nine miles east of here. He was killed shortly thereafter by a strafing fighter. When Leutnant Helmut Kütterer of 7./KG 40 crash-landed four miles northeast of St Jean D'Angely, he and his engineer survived with injuries, but another crewman and two groundcrew were killed.

The last major combat fought between Condors of KG 40 and Allied aircraft commenced in late March and continued into early April. On 27 March convoy JW 58/RA 58 had set sail with 49 ships from Loch Ewe for Murmansk, in the Soviet Union. Amongst the many escort ships accompanying the convoy were two escort carriers, HMS *Tracker* and HMS *Activity*, both with Martlet fighters embarked – 846 NAS on board *Tracker* and 819 NAS on board *Activity*. The convoy was soon detected by the Luftwaffe, which started shadowing it but quickly began to suffer losses. The first was a Ju 88D-1 of 1(F)/22, flown by Feldwebel Walter Kolb, which was shot down by Lts Jack Large and Dick Yeo of 819 NAS, as Yeo recalled;

'Radar picked up a shadower and we were scrambled. After some positioning vectors, we came out of cloud and spotted the enemy aircraft – a Ju 88 – ahead and below. Lt Large went straight in, with me close behind. Bits and pieces flew off in all directions and the enemy aircraft started a diving turn to the right. As Large broke away left, I opened fire at fairly close range. I saw a lot of strikes and a large fire-tinged ball of smoke appeared. I flew through this and my windshield was covered with oil, but it cleared quickly in the slipstream so I was able to get a couple more bursts in. The enemy aircraft was well alight after that and it dived ever steeper and hit the sea almost vertically.'

Despite Large getting tangled up in the German aircraft's trailing aerial, both Wildcats returned safely. However, the position of the convoy had been radioed back, and first thing the following morning Condors were detected in its vicinity. At 0725 hrs Sub-Lts Noel Simon and Alan Swift of 819 NAS were launched to intercept an unidentified aircraft. Simon's account of what ensued read as follows;

'Takeoff from the pitching deck was rather hair-raising, and then for the best part of two hours we were vectored all over the sky at heights ranging from sea level to 10,000 ft. The cloud was so extensive that, although we must have been close to the bandit on more than one occasion, we saw nothing of it. Eventually, with petrol running low and feeling thoroughly frustrated, we were recalled.

'[As we were] approaching the convoy a little below the cloud base, fighter control suddenly piped up urgently with a fresh course to steer. As I turned on to the new heading I spotted the dull grey form of a Condor several miles ahead, flying very low and away from me. Dropping to sea level, I opened up to full throttle, switched on the gunsight and cocked the guns. I flew as low as I dared, virtually skimming the wave tops. The Condor continued on a steady course, but as we drew near it started a gentle turn to port. I was forced to climb slightly to avoid the possibility of Alan Swift hitting the sea. By then the range was closing rapidly and I could not believe that we had not been spotted. We were approaching so fast that at the last moment I had to throttle right back to avoid overshooting.

'Leaving my No 2 to take the port side, I concentrated on the starboard, almost immediately opening fire from astern and slightly below. I was so close the Condor's slipstream caught my aircraft, the turbulence momentarily throwing me off aim, but by then I could hardly miss. I saw my bullets raking the two starboard engines, both of which began to smoke. As they caught fire, the Condor's nose dipped and, almost as though in slow motion, it plunged into the sea in a shower of spray. I had to pull sharply away to avoid following it into the water.'

The Condor crashed at 0920 hrs south of Bear Island. Just over seven hours later a second Condor fell victim to Sub-Lts Gordon Debney and Reg Meed of 846 NAS, breaking up and falling into the sea at 1627 hrs. However, the day did not end there, as *Tracker*'s diary reveals;

'1800 hrs – Lt G B C Sangster and Sub-Lt H Beeston flew off to intercept a bandit. At 1820 hrs they spotted an Fw 200. First its port outer engine was set on fire, then starboard inner and then again the port outer, which had been extinguished. The enemy cartwheeled into the sea and smoke could be seen from the ship.'

It had been a dreadful day for 3./KG 40. Although it is not possible to say who got whom, the C-6 flown by Oberfeldwebel Alfred Weyer, the C-3 flown by Oberleutnant Alfred Klomp and the C-8 flown by Unteroffizier Alfred Göbel were shot down, with the loss of all 20 Condor aircrew. A possible indication of how short 3./KG 40 was of Fw 200s by this stage in the war is the fact that Walter Klomp's aircraft was elderly C-3 Wk-Nr 0062 – 0060 had been lost in action on 19 May 1941, 0061 broke up in mid-air on 15 June 1941, 0063 was damaged in action on 17 July 1941 (and then lost in an accident on 22 February 1942) and 0064 was reported missing on 30 June 1941. It seems that up to 31 March 1944, 0062, and anyone who flew in it, had been lucky.

Although Condor sightings were reported in the following days, no more were lost. However, on the evening of 1 April a Blohm & Voss Bv 138C-1 flying-boat of 3(F)/130, captained by Oberleutnant Kurt Kannengiesser, fell victim to Wildcats flown by Sub-Lt George Willcocks of 846 NAS and Lt John Scott of 819 NAS. The following day, at 1650 hrs, a second Ju 88D-1 of 1(F)/22 (this time flown by Feldwebel Oswald Herpel) was shot down by Lts George Sangster and Wilfred Vittle of 819 NAS.

The three 'Wolfpacks' of U-boats (each with four submarines) targeting the convoy, plus another five additional individual U-boats, fared little better. No ships were hit and the convoy got through unscathed, its escorting vessels and aircraft sinking four U-boats during their defence of the merchantmen. On 29 March U-961 was sunk by HMS *Starling*, on 1 April U-355 was damaged by a Grumman Avenger of 846 NAS and then sunk by HMS *Beagle*, on 2 April U-360 was sunk by HMS *Keppel* and, finally, on 3 April U-288 was sunk by Swordfish of 819 NAS and Avengers of 846 NAS. In total, 202 U-boat crewmen and 34 aircrew died in attacks on this convoy.

Changes now had to occur, as it was clear that Condors could no longer be operated safely in the frontline. On 20 March 1944 III./KG 40 reported that of the 35 Fw 200s on strength, only eight were serviceable. Three months later, although it had only 23 Condors on strength, 12 of them were serviceable. On 1 April 1944 *Fliegerführer Atlantik* was disbanded, with KG 40 and other associated units now coming under X. *Fliegerkorps* control. From this month onwards Condor losses on operations fell to zero, but many aircraft were still being written off and crews killed in accidents. They also continued to fall victim to intruding Allied aircraft.

In May two were lost in accidents, with the deaths of eight crew, followed by another two in June. The worst accident occurred on 14 June when, during a transport flight, Oberfeldwebel Hans Hauenstein's Fw 200C-4 of 9./KG 40 hit a tree while landing at Roth, in Germany, killing ten air- and groundcrew and injuring two. Intruders were also active on a number of occasions in late June and early July. On the evening of 22 June a Condor crew from *Stab* III./KG 40 almost fell victim to two Mosquitoes from No 151 Sqn (callsigns 'Snoozy 34' and 'Snoozy 41'), as the combat report of Flt Lt Len Gregory related;

'We sighted a large aircraft about three to four miles away, dead ahead on a southerly course. We were closing range rapidly when the aircraft turned on to an easterly course, at the same time lowering its undercarriage. It then became evident that the aircraft intended to land at Cognac, so we increased speed. By the time range had closed sufficiently for an attack to be carried out, the aircraft, which was identified as an Fw 200, was well on the approach run. "Snoozy 34" [Flg Offs B C Gray and L T Gorvon] gave a three-second burst. Strikes were seen on port mid-fuselage.

'"Snoozy 41" gave a two- to three-second burst from 1500 yards range. Enemy aircraft's height below 50 ft – four to five strikes seen on port outer engine. Enemy aircraft continued to touch down and run along the runway quite normally. Fairly intense flak had opened up on us, and we carried on to the next objective.'

Damage to the Condor was slight, but it did result in the death of Flieger Ingenieur Anton Wagner.

The final Condor to fall victim to an intruder in France was claimed on 5 July, and experienced radio operator Feldwebel Otto Kipp was a part of its crew. His operational flying had started with He 111s of 8./KG 40 in the summer of 1941, his pilot being Leutnant Herbert Fobker (who was killed in a bombing raid on Cognac on 31 December 1943). Kipp subsequently flew with III./KG 40's Feldwebel Heinz Grauber until they were down by the intruder on 5 July 1944. Kipp's account of this fateful flight read as follows;

'We were ordered to fly to an auxiliary airfield located at the so-called Charentes meadows. This was so the aircraft would be protected from the daily fighter-bomber attacks. We took off early in the morning – we had been told there were no enemy aircraft in our airspace. However, this proved to be wrong, and we were attacked by a Lightning just after takeoff at an altitude of 160 ft. Our aeroplane burst into flames, so we had to make an emergency landing in a cornfield where farmers were harvesting.'

The Condor's attacker was Capt Art Jeffrey of the 434th FS/479nd FG, who was flying one of 13 P-38s from the 434th that had arrived over Cognac just after 0900 hrs. Once the pilots had spotted the Fw 200 taking off the end result was inevitable, as Jeffrey's combat report shows;

'My right wingman called over the radio that a plane was taking off. Since my Flight was closest, I called Newcross Leader to furnish top cover while I went down for a pass. The plane had made a 180-degree turn to port and was staying on the deck, close to the airdrome and town. There was quite a lot of flak being shot at us from this area. I came at the enemy aircraft from the front, making a 180-degree overhead pass and setting up for a stern shot at him. I began firing at about 350 yards, closing to about 50 yards [and] giving him about a ten-second burst. The right inboard engine caught fire immediately and parts flew off it. The pilot then made a belly landing, and by the time the ship had stopped skidding the whole plane was ablaze. I observed one man making his escape from the front of the ship.'

Amazingly, half of the crew emerged from the rear of the burning Condor without injury, and the three that were injured, including Kipp, were only lightly wounded. Sadly, mechanic Unteroffizier Otto Kiphut had been killed by a single bullet to the head, however.

The skies over northwest Europe were clearly becoming a dangerous place for Condors. As Fw 200s were unable to operate over the Atlantic from French bases following the Allied invasion of Normandy on 6 June 1944, the following month the decision was made to withdraw them from France to Norway, Germany or Austria. Thenceforth, Condors were used entirely in the transport role, as it was all but impossible to carry out effective combat sorties with any guarantee of success, or of a safe return for the crews involved. Nonetheless, losses still occurred, with three aircraft being written off in accidents in July. On the 9th Leutnant Helmut Kütterer of 7./KG 40 crashed into a mountain at St Nicholas des Biefs, northeast of Clermont Ferrand, while on a ferry flight, resulting in the death of 12 air- and groundcrew. Nine days later Oberleutnant Eduard Zöschling of 12./KG 40 crashed between Libourne and Mirambeau, in southwestern France, shortly after takeoff on another ferry flight, killing nine more air- and groundcrew.

Meanwhile, in Norway, III./KG 40 was still attempting to operate as an effective unit. On 14 August experienced pilot Oberleutnant Rudolf Biberger, now the *Gruppenadjutant* of III./KG 40, was trying to introduce a new crew from 8./KG 40 to flying in and around Trondheim when their Condor hit the ground during a turn after it was probably caught in an air stream coming off a mountain.

Despite all the doom and gloom surrounding the Condor, there were the occasional successes. Oberleutnant Karl-Heinz Stahnke, a highly experienced transport pilot, had transferred to 3./KG 40 in the spring of 1943. As well as carrying out normal Condor missions, as an accomplished pilot he was also tasked with performing reconnaissance and resupply flights to weather stations in the Polar region. One such weather station, named *Schatzgräber* (Treasure Hunter), was located on Alexandra Land, the most westerly island of Franz-Josef Land, and had been in operation since September 1943. In early July 1944 it was discovered that nine of the ten-man detachment had fallen very ill with trichinosis as a result of eating polar bear meat.

The ice prevented seaplanes or boats from reaching them, so on 7 July Stahnke took off from Banak, in northern Norway, and, after an eight-hour flight, decided to land on what appeared to be a suitable area three miles from the weather station. This he did, but not without incident. The inner tyre of the starboard undercarriage and the tailwheel were damaged, and at the end of the landing run the Condor ran into a dip that caused it to tip onto its nose and drop back again, after which it sank up to its axles in melting ice. Despite this, a party from the aeroplane, including a doctor, made it to the weather station and began treating the sick.

Stahnke now faced the problem of returning home. On 8 July a Blohm & Voss Bv 222 flying-boat dropped spares to enable the Condor to be repaired, and for the next two days, under trying circumstances, the crew not only fixed the aircraft but also created an obstacle-free runway. Finally, in a hair-raising takeoff, the Condor plus passengers managed to get airborne during the evening of 10 July, landing without incident at Banak the next morning. The Condor crew were greeted as heroes and Stahnke was awarded the *Ritterkreuz* on 24 October 1944.

However, such successes were few and far between. The last Condor to be shot down fell on 27 September. Its pilot, Flugkapitän Helmut Liman, had been a pre-war aviator with *DLH* prior to transferring to the Luftwaffe upon the outbreak of war. Having flown operationally with 7./KG 40 (he took part on the attack on convoy 'Faith' in July 1943), Liman transferred back to *DLH*. On 27 September he was making a passenger flight from Stuttgart to Spain in veteran Fw 200D-2 Wk-Nr 0021, registered D-AMHL and named *Pommern*, when, at 2031 hrs, the Condor was intercepted by a Beaufighter nightfighter of No 415 Sqn, crewed by Capt Harold Augspurger and 2Lt Austin Petry, which shot it down. The aeroplane crashed at St Nicholas les Citeaux, just south of Dijon, where the Beaufighter was based. The crew of three and five passengers were all killed.

For the remaining eight months of the war in Europe Condors were all but extinct. Surviving examples now performed those duties for which the aircraft had originally been designed, namely transport, but losses still occurred. The worst of these was on 11 October when a Condor of 7./KG 40 flown by Leutnant Hans Gilbert crashed into

In this dramatic camera-gun film photograph taken by a Beaufighter of No 252 Sqn on 31 March 1945, Oberleutnant Stahnke's Fw 200 G6+AY is just visible under camouflaged netting and tree branches. Six Beaufighters had targeted Calato airfield, on the Greek island of Rhodes, after an RAF photo-reconnaissance aircraft had spotted the Condor, an He 111 and a Ju 52/3m. None of the No 252 Sqn aircrew spotted the Fw 200 during the attack, however, thanks to its effective concealment

Lavangerjjord, south of Bardufoss. The cause of this accident was attributed to structural failure due to the aircraft being overloaded – it was carrying five crew and 46 passengers, 41 of which were German female auxiliaries. There were no survivors. Then, ten days later, Oberfeldwebel Wolfgang Liepe of 7./KG 40 crashed on takeoff from Nautsi on the Norway/Finland/Russian border on another transport flight. Three crew, including Liepe, were killed and three injured.

In November KG 40 was disbanded (in over-optimistic preparation for the formation of the Messerschmitt Me 262-equipped KG(*Jagd*) 40), and its aircraft, air- and groundcrew were dispersed to other units. Re-designated *Transportfliegerstaffel Condor*, 8./KG 40 was commanded by Hauptmann Ludwig Progner, formerly of 7./KG 40. Some aircraft were transferred to 14./*Transportgeschwader* 4 at Wiener-Neustadt, in Austria, where two Condors formed a *Sonderkommando*, led by Oberleutnant Karl-Heinz Stahnke – the pilot of the other aircraft was Oberfeldwebel Adalbert Schraffanek. This *Sonderkommando*'s claim to fame was that the last recorded RAF 'combat' with a Condor (albeit the aircraft was on the ground and the results were inconclusive) was between Beaufighters of No 252 Sqn and this unit.

The Allies had become aware of regular transport flights by Condors of the *Sonderkommando* between Wiener-Neustadt or Horsching, in Austria, and Calato airfield on the Greek island of Rhodes. The precise purpose of their missions (the first of which was recorded by the Allies on 28 January 1945) was unknown, but it was thought that they were part of preparations for an attack on the Suez Canal using Hs 293s.

At 2345 hrs on 30 March Stahnke, who had been awarded the *Eichenlaub* to his *Ritterkreuz* three days before, took off for Calato from Wiener-Neustadt in Condor G6+AY. He arrived just before dawn on 31 March, when his aircraft, together with an He 111 and a Ju 52/3m, was spotted by a photo-reconnaissance aircraft. Six Beaufighters of No 252 Sqn, based at Hassani, in Greece, and led by Sqn Ldr Tony Hunter, took off at 1450 hrs with the intention of destroying the German aircraft on Calato. This was not the first time No 252 Sqn had been after a Condor on Calato. On 17 March 1945 Flg Off Doug Reid and Flg Off Ron Ray carried out a first-light reconnaissance of the island looking for Stahnke's Condor, which had arrived two days earlier. They saw nothing, so the Condor must have been well camouflaged, as it did not take off for Austria until the following day.

On arriving at Calato in two formations of three, the Beaufighter crews again saw nothing, so they promptly attacked buildings on the airfield instead. They encountered moderate to light AA fire, interspersed with the occasional heavy flak burst, which damaged the tail of Flg Off J K Underwood's Beaufighter, the nose of Flt Sgt L G Armitage's aircraft and the undercarriage of Flg Off Bill Escreet's machine, bursting a tyre. Despite this, all six landed safely and, on developing camera-gun film taken by Flg Off Doug Reid, there to everyone's great annoyance was the Condor, cleverly camouflaged under

The Stahnke crew at Trondheim-Værnes on 8 April 1944. A highly experienced transport pilot, Oberleutnant Karl-Heinz Stahnke (seen here third from right) had transferred to 3./KG 40 in the spring of 1943. As well as carrying out normal Condor missions, as an accomplished pilot he was also tasked with performing reconnaissance and resupply flights to weather stations in the Polar region

olive trees. Stahnke took off that evening, and at the end of the war the Allies discovered G6+FY, together with Adalbert Schraffanek and his crew, at Calato, where they had arrived on 3 May.

OTHER MAJOR UNITS

Appendix 1 lists all units that operated the Condor. From a combat perspective the major

Formerly D-ACVH *Grenzmark* with *DLH* but now Fw 200A-0 Wk-Nr 3098 NK+NM of the *FdF*, this aeroplane was destroyed in a crash-landing at Orel, in the Soviet Union, on 23 December 1941

users were only I. and III./KG 40, with IV./KG 40 being the designated training *Gruppe*. The only other military operator, not including *DLH*, was *Fliegerstaffel des Führers (FdF)*. Condors assigned to *FdF* were actively used by senior political and military personages from Hitler downwards (curiously, Reichsmarschall Hermann Göring was an exception, preferring to travel by train).

Three Condors from *FdF* were captured at the end of the war and taken to the Royal Aircraft Establishment at Farnborough. Reichsführer Heinrich Himmler's Fw 200C-4/U1 was of considerable interest as it had accommodation for 11 passengers. Himmler had a private compartment facing forward on the starboard side, and this was armour plated, including a moveable sheet of armour that could be positioned to counter a threat from any particular direction. It also had a personal escape window, a folding wooden table and a bookcase. Of limited use to the RAF, all three Condors, assigned Air Ministry numbers 94, 95 and 97 (Air Ministry 96 was Fw 200C-4 Wk-Nr 0111, registered D-ASVX, formerly of *DLH* and given to Danish airline *DDL*), were essentially used for static evaluation and exhibition. However, surplus to requirements in post-war Britain, they were soon scrapped.

POSTSCRIPT

At war's end, Condors were found scattered across airfields. As with those of the *FdF*, they were quickly disposed of. A number were found to be in flying condition, including Fw 200C-5/FK F8+FS of *Transportfliegerstaffel Condor*, which was meant to have been flown from Trondheim-Værnes to the besieged Courland Pocket, in Latvia, on a transport flight on 8 May 1945 by an Oberfeldwebel Bergen, who wisely diverted to Wuppertal instead and landed at Achmer, in Germany. It is believed that this aircraft, still bearing the code F8+FS but now with RAF roundels, was seen at Melsbroek, in Belgium, but its eventual fate is unknown.

On the same day (8 May), Unteroffizier Harald Loseke of *Transportfliegerstaffel Condor* landed Fw 200C-3/U1 Wk-Nr 0191, coded F8+MS, at Torslanda, in

Fw 200 V-3 Wk-Nr 3099 26+00 *Immelmann III* of the *FdF* started life as Focke-Wulf Flugzeugbau's ninth production aircraft and initially flew with *DLH* as D-ARHU, named *Ostmark*. In January 1939 it became Hitler's personal transport aircraft, being recoded D-2600 and then WL+2600 and renamed *Immelmann III*. In November 1939 the Condor joined the *FdF* and was recoded 26+00. It remained with the *FdF*, flying Hitler and other senior Nazi dignitaries on countless occasions until it was destroyed in an air raid on 18 July 1944.

Minister of Armaments and War Production Albert Speer stands (third from right) in front of his personal Fw 200C-6/U2 Wk-Nr 0216 TA+MR in the winter of 1942-43. Assigned to the *FdF*, this aeroplane was destroyed in a strafing attack on Schönwalde on 10 April 1945

Fw 200C-4/U2 Wk-Nr 0181 GC+SJ of the *FdF* was the personal Condor of Grossadmiral Karl Dönitz (note the U-boat marking on the forward fuselage). It was captured at Flensburg and became AIR MIN 97. The aeroplane crashed on takeoff from Schleswig on 28 February 1946 and was subsequently scrapped

Sweden, with six crew/passengers from both *Transportfliegerstaffel Condor* and the reconnaissance unit 1(F)/22. This aircraft was scrapped in 1948.

Before the last Condor had been delivered, in the summer of 1944, the Luftwaffe had received about 252 examples (276 had been built). However, only one almost complete Condor exists today, although the wreckage of a number of Fw 200s can be found in Scandinavia. On 22 February 1942 Oberleutnant Karl Thiede of 7./KG 40 ditched Fw 200C-3 Wk-Nr 0063 in Storsdalsfjord, and significant pieces of the aircraft were recovered in May 1999 and can now be seen under restoration at the *Deutsches Technikmuseum* in Berlin.

Although a brilliant and iconic pre-war airliner, the Condor had serious failings as a combat aircraft. Yet there was no credible alternative initially, and even when that alternative, in the form of the He 177, arrived, it too proved to be not as good as intended. Thus the Condor was forced to fill a gap in the Luftwaffe's arsenal. For a year from the end of the Battle of Britain until the summer of 1941, despite suffering dreadful serviceability problems – something that plagued the aircraft throughout its life – the Condor's reputation and abilities preceded it. However, its abilities were seriously brought into question as the war progressed and Allied defences and superiority improved.

Winston Churchill said, 'To the U-boat scourge was now added air attack far out in the oceans by long-range aircraft. Of these, the Focke-Wulf 200, known as the Condor, was the most formidable'. As a result of this statement, post-war historians have dubbed the aircraft the 'Scourge of the Atlantic'. For the part it played in the Battle of the Atlantic, albeit limited in duration and latterly in impact, the Condor will never be forgotten.

Fw 200C-5/FK F8+FS of *Transportfliegerstaffel Condor* was captured intact at Achmer on 8 April 1945 and repainted in RAF markings. The aircraft was then possibly flown by its new owners, as the Condor was reportedly seen at Melsbroek, in Belgium. The Fw 200's ultimate fate is not known, but it must have eventually been scrapped

APPENDICES

APPENDIX 1

Fw 200 CONDOR UNITS – SENIOR EXECUTIVE OFFICERS

Compiled and provided by KG 40 *Archiv Günther Ott, Arbeitsgemeinschaft Deutsche Luftfahrthistorik (ADL)* – German Aviation History Working Group, Potsdam/Germany

KG 40
Kommodore

Oberstleutnant/Oberst Hans Geisse	7/40 to 7/9/40	Killed 7/9/40
Oberst Ernst-August Roth	7/40 to 12/40	Disbanded (to KG 28)
Major Edgar Petersen	4/41 to 9/41	To *KdE* Rechlin
Oberstleutnant Dr Georg Pasewaldt	10/41 to 12/41	To KG 2
Oberst Karl Mehnert	1/42 to 7/42	To *RdL/ObdL*
Oberst Martin Vetter	9/42 to 8/43	To *RdL/ObdL*
Major Robert Kowalewski	8/43 to 8/43	To *RdL/ObdL*
Oberstleutnant/Oberst Rupprecht Heyn	9/43 to 9/44	To *Stab* X. *Fliegerkorps*
Oberstleutnant Hanns Heise	11/44 to 2/45	Disbanded

I./KG 40*
Gruppenkommandeur

Hauptmann/Major Edgar Petersen	5/40 to 11/4	To *LW-Führungsstab*
Hauptmann Fritz Fliegel	11/40 to 18/7/41	Killed in Action
Hauptmann/Major Edmund Daser	8/41 to 7/42	To *E-Stelle* Rechlin
Major Karl Henkelmann	7/42 to 9/44	To OKL/Chef TLR
Hauptmann Siegfried Frhr von Cramm	11/44 to 2/45	Disbanded

(*Converts to He 177, only 3. *Staffel* continued with Fw 200 until disbanded 7/44 and aircraft transferred to III./KG 40. Converts to Me 262 11/44 to 2/45 – not completed)

III./KG 40*
Gruppenkommandeur

Major Walther Herbold	4/41 to 7/41	To I./GKS 1
Hauptmann/Major Robert Kowalewski	7/41 to 8/43	To *Stab.*/KG 40
Hauptmann Walter Rieder	9/43 to 12/43	To II./KG 40
Hauptmann/Major Dr Lambert Konschegg	12/43 to 11/44	To *Stab/Luftflotte Reich* von Pramburg
Hauptmann Joachim Ohm	12/44 to 2/45	Disbanded

(*Converts from He 111 11/41-5/42. Converts to Me 262 12/44 to 2/45 – not completed)

IV./KG 40*
Gruppenkommandeur

Hauptmann/Major Roman Dawczynski	9/41 to 9/4	To *Fl H Kdtr Biblis*
Oberstleutnant Walter Junghanns	11/44 to 2/45	Disbanded

(*Converts to Me 262 12/44 to 2/45 – not completed)

II./KG 40 and V./KG 40
Did not fly Fw 200

KG 40 RELATED UNITS

KGrzbV 200
Gruppenkommandeur

Major Hans-Jürgen Willers   1/43 to 3/43   To *Kdo Willers*/KG 40
(*Kommando Willers*/KG 40 reduced to *Staffel* size as 2./KG 40 and integrated into III./KG 40 3/43, renamed 8./KG 40 11/43)

Transportfliegerstaffel Condor (formerly 8./KG 40)
Staffelkapitän

Hauptmann Ludwig Progner 11/44 to 4/45   Disbanded

Condor-Aufklärungsschwarm
Bardufoss/Trondheim (reporting to 1(F)/130)

Schwarmführer

Leutnant Hans-Joachim Graefe	1/45 to 5/45	Disbanded (7 aircraft)

Sonderkommando Condor (on detachment from 14./TG 4 to Lwkdo 4)
Kommandoführer

Oberstleutnant Karl-Heinz Stahnke	1/45 to 5/45	Disbanded (2 aircraft)

OTHER UNITS

1./*Fernaufklärungsgruppe* 120 (1.(F)/120)
Staffelkapitän

Hauptmann Helmut Orlowski   8/42 to 12/42   (4 aircraft)

1./*Fernaufklärungsgruppe* 122 (1.(F)/122)
Staffelkapitän

Hauptmann Kurt Junghans   12/42 to 1/43   (1 aircraft)

10.(*Sonderstaffel*)/KGzbV 172
Staffelkapitän

Hauptmann Otto Brauer   9/39 to 10/39   (1 aircraft)

4./KGrzbV 107 *Staffelkapitän*

Hauptmann Hans Josef Reichel   3/40 to 6/40   Disbanded (7 aircraft)

2./KGrzbV 108
Staffelkapitän

Hauptmann Hans Josef Reichel   6/40   (1 aircraft)

Blindflugschule 6
Kommandeur

Major Hans Josef Reichel   6/42 to 10/42   (1 aircraft)

Fliegerstaffel des Führers (FdF)
Kommandeur

Oberst/Generalleutnant d Pol Hans   9/39 to 4/45   To *Kuriergruppe*
Baur   *OKW*

Kuriergruppe OKW
Gruppenkommandeur

Major Erich Adam   5/45 to 5/45   Disbanded
(3 aircraft)

Versuchsstelle für Höhenflüge (VfH – Sonderformation der Aufkl.Gr. Ob.d.L.) Gruppenkommandeur

Oberstleutnant Theodor Rowehl   8/39 to 3/40   (4 aircraft)

2./Versuchsverband Ob.d.L
Staffelkapitän

Major Karl-Edmund Gartenfeld   10/43 to 11/43   (2 aircraft)

APPENDIX 2

I., III. AND IV./KG 40 *RITTERKREUZ* HOLDERS

Name	Unit(s)	Award Date	Notes
Oberstleutnant Hans Buchholz	I./KG 40	24/3/41	Killed 19/5/41
Hauptmann Edmund Daser	I. and IV./KG 40	21/2/41	
Hauptmann Fritz Fliegel	I./KG 40	25/3/41	Killed 18/7/41
Oberstleutnant Hanns Heise	*Stab*./KG 40	3/9/42	With I./KG 76
Oberleutnant Ernst Hetzel	*Stab* I./KG 40	24/4/45	Awarded after KG 40
Oberleutnant Bernhard Jope	2./KG 40	30/10/40	*Eichenlaub* 24/3/44 with KG 100
Oberstleutnant Dr Lambert von Konschegg	*Stab*./KG 40	28/2/45	
Major Robert Kowalewski	*Stab* III./KG 40	24/11/40	With II./KG 26
Hauptmann Herbert Kunt	12./KG 40	14/3/43	With KG 100
Hauptmann Albrecht Kuntze	12./KG 40	16/5/40	With KG 26 and killed 5/7/43
Hauptmann Rudolf Mayr	9./KG 40	18/5/43	
Oberleutnant Rudolf Mons	I./KG 40	18/9/41	Killed 26/11/43 with II./KG 40
Major Edgar Petersen	I./KG 40	21/10/40	
Oberleutnant Heinrich Schlosser	I./KG 40	18/9/41	
Oberleutnant Karl-Heinz Stahnke	3./KG 40	24/10/44	*Eichenlaub* 27/3/45
Oberst Martin Vetter	KG 40	16/5/40	With KG 26

APPENDIX 3

AIRCREW AWARDED THE *DEUTSCHES KREUZ* IN GOLD WHILE WITH I. AND III./KG 40

Name	Crew Position	Award Date	Notes
Stab			
Oberstleutnant Georg Pasewaldt	Pilot	27/7/42	
Hauptmann Dr Lambert von Konschegg	Pilot	8/2/43	
I. Gruppe			
Major Edmund Daser	Pilot	25/6/42	
Hauptmann Bernhard Jope	Pilot	5/2/42	
Oberleutnant Robert Maly	Pilot	24/6/43	
Leutnant Rudolf Mayr	Pilot	23/12/41	
Major Ernst Pflüger	Pilot	1/2/43	
1. Staffel			
Leutnant Wilhelm Dette	Pilot	14/4/42	PoW with 9./KG 40 28/12/43
Leutnant Otto Gose	Pilot	25/2/42	Killed 22/5/44
Oberfeldwebel Herbert Preiss	Radio Operator	24/6/43	
2. Staffel			
Oberfeldwebel Wilhelm Blume	Radio Operator	27/11/42	
Leutnant Oskar Graf	Pilot	25/9/42	
Oberfeldwebel Fritz Kühn	Pilot	25/9/42	Killed 14/8/42
Oberfeldwebel Wilhelm Zeyer	Pilot	20/10/42	
3. Staffel			
Feldwebel Gerhard Dörschel	Flight Engineer	8/9/42	
Oberfeldwebel Gerhard Langer	Flight Engineer	31/8/43	
Oberfeldwebel Hellmuth Schumann	Radio Operator	2/7/42	
Oberfeldwebel Gustav Spieth	Radio Operator	17/10/43	
Oberleutnant Karl Waterbeck	Pilot	25/11/43	Killed 21/1/44
Oberleutnant Reinhold Wrede	Pilot	24/2/44	
III. Gruppe			
Oberfeldwebel Wolfgang Gierke	Radio Operator	19/5/43	
Oberfeldwebel Paul Henze	Flight Engineer	21/8/42	
Major Robert Kowalewski	Pilot	2/7/42	
Oberleutnant Joachim Ohm	Pilot	17/10/43	
Major Helmut Liman	Pilot	?	
7. Staffel			
Oberleutnant Ludwig Progner	Pilot	17/10/43	
8. Staffel			
Stabsfeldwebel Dirk Höfkes	Pilot	21/8/42	PoW 30/7/42
Oberfeldwebel Johann Rosenheimer	Flight Engineer	5/2/44	
9. Staffel			
Oberleutnant Herbert Fobker	Pilot	17/10/43	Killed 31/12/43

APPENDIX 4

I./KG 40 SHIPPING CLAIMS 10 JULY TO 31 OCTOBER 1940

Date	Details	Bombs	Location	Fate
13/8/40	Freighter 8000T 1400 hrs	1 x SC 250	100 km NNE Ireland	Damaged
18/8/40	Freighter 2000T (*Svein Jarl* 1250 hrs)	6 x SC 250	50 km west of Valentia, Ireland	Damaged
20/8/40	Freighter 12,000T (Possibly SS *Macville*)	2 x SD 250	southwest of Blacksod, Co Mayo	Damaged
25/8/40	Freighter 3821T (SS *Goathland*)	3 x SC 250	630 km west of Lands End	Sunk
10/9/40	Freighter 8000T 0930 hrs (Possibly SS *Clan Lamont*)	?	damaged 60 miles north of Malin Head	Damaged
12/9/40	Freighter 8000T (Possibly SS *Tintern Abbey*)		40 km southwest Isle of Man	Damaged
14/9/40	Freighter 8000 T Possibly SS *West Kedron*	4 x SC 250	attacked 30 miles northeast of Malin Head	Sunk
16/9/40	15,000T 0030 hrs	2 x SC 250	Rathlin Island	Damaged
17/9/40	Freighter 5152T (SS *Kalliope* 0830 hrs)	1 x SC 250	west of Londonderry	Sunk
24/9/40	Cruiser 0650 hrs	4 x SC 250	15W/6675	Damaged
27/9/40	Cargo ship 6000T (SS *Ascero* 1015 hrs)	4 x SC 250	210 km northwest of Carndonah	Sunk
30/9/40	Cargo ship 10,000T (Possibly SS *Baron Vernon*)	2 x SC 250	attacked 290 miles west of Valentia	Sunk
2/10/40	Cargo ship 2300T (SS *Latymer*) [Oberleutnant Schlosser 2./KG 40]	1 x SC 250	southwest point of Ireland	Sunk
8/10/40	Transporter 20,043T (SS *Oronsay* 1100 hrs)	4 x SC 250	230 km west of Tiree	Damaged
11/10/40	Cargo ship 8000T 1140 hrs [Oberleutnant Schuldt 2./KG 40] (Possibly SS *Empire Audacity*)	SW Heb	400 miles northwest of Malin Head	Damaged
12/10/40	Freighter 4000T	?	off Iona	Sunk
26/10/40	*Empress of Britain* [Oberleutnant Jope 2./KG 40]	6 x SC 250 2 x SC 250	60 miles west of Donegal Bay	Damaged
27/10/40	Cargo ship 8000T 1050 hrs (Possibly SS *Alfred Jones* or SS *Balzac*)	2 x SC 250	northwest Burtonport	Damaged
31/10/40	Cargo ship 5700T 1100 hrs (SS *Starstone*) [Feldwebel Flinsch 2./KG 40]	2 x SC 250	300 km west of Achil Head	Sunk

APPENDIX 5

Fw 200s USED BY *FLIEGERSTAFFEL DES FÜHRERS* (FDF)

Variant	Wk-Nr	Code	Details
Fw 200A-0	3098	NK+NM	Destroyed in crash-landing, Orel, 23/12/41
Fw 200 V3	3099	26+00	Destroyed in air raid 18/7/44
Fw 200C-3U9	0099	KE+IX	Unknown
Fw 200C-4/U1	0137	CE+IB	Personal aircraft of Adolf Hitler. Shot down by Soviet fighter at Petrika, near Lodz, 24/8/44
Fw 200C-4/U2	0138	CE+IC	Crashed Wilhelmsdorf, near Potsdam, 27/4/45
Fw 200C-4/U1	0176	GC+AE	Personal aircraft of Heinrich Himmler. Captured Flensburg. Became AIR MIN 94
Fw 200C-4/U2	0181	GC+SJ	Personal aircraft of Karl Dönitz. Captured Flensburg. Became AIR MIN 97 Due to be delivered to *DDL* but crashed on takeoff from Schleswig on 28/2/46 and subsequently scrapped

Fw 200C-6/U2	0216	TA+MR	Personal aircraft of Albert Speer. Destroyed in strafing attack, Schönwalde, 10/4/45
Fw 200C-6/U2	0230	DP+OR	Senior officer transport, fate unknown
Fw 200C-4/U1	0240	TK+CV	Personal aircraft of Adolf Hitler. Captured Flensburg. Became AIR MIN 95

APPENDIX 6

STANDARD Fw 200C MILITARY VARIANTS (*UMRÜSTSÄTZE*)

Gun Position	Designations:
A-Stand	Front dorsal
B-Stand	Rear dorsal
C-Stand	Rear ventral
D-Stand	Front ventral
F-Stand	Beam guns port and starboard

C-0 – Pre-production batch of ten aircraft, structural strengthening. Four were manufactured as unarmed transports, the remainder were fitted with three MG 15s. BMW 132H engines.

C-1 – First military production version from summer 1940, fitted with full-length ventral gondola which allowed for a narrow bomb-bay. Armament of MG 15 in *B-Stand*, MG 15 in *C-Stand*, MG FF in *D-Stand* and 2100 kg bomb load.

C-2 – Similar to C-1 but with a recessed underside to the rear of each of the two outboard engine nacelles which reduced drag and could carry a 250 kg bomb.

C-3 – Structurally strengthened, powered by Bramo 323 R-2 radial engines. *A-Stand* MG 15 and later MG 131, *B-Stand* MG 15 and later MG 13, *C-Stand* MG 15, *D-Stand* MG/FF or MG 15, *F-Stand* two MG 15s. Bomb load of 1230 kg (full fuel load) and 5400 kg max (with reduced range).

C-3/U4 – Radio modifications. Armoured long-range tanks. Crew of seven. *A-Stand* MG 15 or MG 131, *B-Stand* MG 131, *C-Stand* MG 15, *D-Stand* MG 151, *F-Stand* two MG 15s. Bomb load of 1030 kg (full fuel load) and 5400 kg max (with reduced range).

C-3/U5 – MG 151 in *A-Stand*.

C-3/U6 – Field conversion for increased armament.

C-3/U7 – Experimental carrier for *Kehl* III.

C-3/U8 – Improved armament and additional fuel tanks.

C-3/U9 – Armed transport.

C-4 – As C-3.

C-4/U1 – Armed VIP tranpsort.

C-4/U2 – Armed VIP transport.

C-4/U3 – Rostock or FuG 200 Hohentwiel ASV. MG 151 in *B1-Stand*, MG 131 in *B2-Stand*, MG 15 in *C-Stand*, MG 151 in *D-Stand*, MG 15 in two side windows. Improved range and altitude.

C-5/U1 – Changes to *B-Stand*.

C-5/U2 – As C-4 but with reinforced armour plating.

C-6 – As C-3 or C-4. Modified to carry Hs 293.

C-8 – Fitted with FuG 200 Hohentwiel ASV, equipped with FuG 203b Kehl III missile control transmitter and fitted with Hs 293 missiles.

APPENDIX 7

CONDOR ATTACK PROFILE

A typical sortie from Bordeaux-Mérignac would see the crew rising at around midnight, eating a meal and then heading to a target briefing. Usually sorties were directed toward known convoy routes where either U-boats or the Kriegsmarine's *B-Dienst* (intelligence service) had detected recent traffic, although the information could be 12 to 24 hours old by the time the crew received it.

Unlike a standard bomber mission against a fixed target, the Condor was generally assigned a search area where either moving convoys or independently steaming ships were expected to pass through. While the *Beobachter* (observer) plotted the appropriate course, the groundcrews finished fuelling and arming the aeroplane. If more than one Fw 200 was involved in the mission, crews would coordinate their search zones to cover the maximum amount of area near the suspected convoy.

In darkness the aircraft would take off and head toward the convoy routes. Usually the Condor would reach its search area in about six hours after a long and usually uneventful flight over the Atlantic. In 1940-41 there was little or no risk of enemy interception, but by mid-1942 crews had to be alert for enemy air activity. During the outbound leg, Condors generally flew in radio silence, even if operating with several aircraft. Finding convoys or independent ships could be far more difficult than expected. Convoys could be difficult to spot, particularly in adverse weather conditions over the Atlantic.

Once a Condor arrived in its target area, as many of the crew as possible would scan the sea for vessels while the pilots flew several search legs through the target area. If multiple aircraft were involved in the mission, they would split up at this point to cover their individual areas. Typical endurance in the search area was initially about three to four hours, but this was extended as improved Fw 200 models arrived in 1941. If a convoy or another significant target was spotted, the pilots would usually manoeuvre closer, using clouds for concealment as much as possible, and observe the target. The *Bordfunker* (radio operator) would break radio silence to vector in other Condors if they were nearby so as to mount a coordinated attack.

During this observation phase, which could last up to an hour, the crew would try to identify the escorts, if any, as well as the best targets to attack. Ideally, the Fw 200 sought its victims from stragglers, minimising the risk of defensive fire. Early Condors were not fitted with an effective bombsight, which meant that strikes had to generally be carried out at low level. Generalleutnant Martin Harlinghausen, who was the first *Fliegerführer Atlantik*, developed the 'Swedish Turnip' or skip bombing attack method with X. *Fliegerkorps*, which entailed approaching the target from abeam at a height of 45-50 m and then releasing the bombs about 300-400 m short of the target. The bombs would head towards the target, hopefully striking at the waterline. This method offered a higher probability of a hit, but also exposed the Condor to the vessel's AA defences (if it was equipped with any).

Although I./KG 40 used the 'Swedish Turnip' attack method almost exclusively in 1940-41, many pilots preferred the safer approach of attacking from dead astern. From that angle the chances of a hit were reduced, but it was safer for the Condor as ships normally carried their AA guns toward the bow. Just in case, most Fw 200s would use their ventral machine guns or 20 mm cannon to strafe the decks in order to suppress any gunners. Normally, a Condor would make several passes on a target, dropping only one or two bombs each time. As it overflew, hopefully not taking too much AA fire, the pilots would pull up sharply and turn around for another pass, or shift to another target. Once all bombs were dropped the Condor would head back to either Bordeaux-Mérignac or to Trondheim-Værnes. From the latter base, the crew would subsequently return to France in order to undertake another sortie.

APPENDIX 8

SELECTED BIOGRAPHIES

Fritz Fliegel

Born in Berlin in 1907, Fliegel qualified as a pilot in 1931 and joined the Army three years later. However, in January 1935 he transferred to the Luftwaffe as a Leutnant and soon became an instructor at a series of flying schools, starting in Celle, where he taught blind-flying. Promoted to Hauptmann on 1 March 1939, Fliegel was sent to II./KG 158 at Wiener-Neustadt, in Austria, as a *Staffelkapitän* – the unit was re-designated II./KG 77 in May 1939. It is believed that he then flew combat missions over Poland. On 8 May 1940 Fliegel was posted to I./KG 40, becoming *Staffelkapitän* of 2./KG 40. He flew missions from Germany and Denmark, and following the fall of France moved with the unit to Bordeaux-Mérignac for the impending offensive against Allied vessels sailing in the Atlantic. In November 1940 he took command of I./KG 40 from Major Edgar Petersen, and on 25 March 1941 he was awarded the *Ritterkreuz*.

Fritz Fliegel received two mentions in German propaganda releases. The first, dated 10 February 1941, reports an attack on a convoy 500 km west of the Portuguese coast by Condors led by him that resulted in the sinking of a 24,500 BRT freighter and the damaging of four more ships. The report further states that from 1 August 1940, I./KG 40 had either sunk or damaged 85 ships totalling 363,500 BRT. A further report dated 20 June 1941 notes that under the leadership of Major Edgar Petersen and then Fritz Fliegel, I./KG 40 had sunk 109 ships and damaged another 63 from mid-April 1940. There are no further mentions of Fliegel, as just under a month after the last report he was killed.

On 18 July 1941 he and his crew (Leutnant Wolf-Dietrich Kadelke, Oberfeldwebel Johannes Rottke, Gefreiter Karl Becker and Unteroffiziers Johann Kothe and Karl Meurer) took off in Fw 200C-3 Wk-Nr 0043, coded F8+AB. It is believed that Fliegel found and attacked convoy OB 346 (which had departed Liverpool four days earlier, bound for Freetown), but the Condor suffered a direct hit by AA fire that ripped off its wing. This lucky shot was fired either by the armed merchantmen SS *Norman Prince* (sunk by U-156 on 29 May 1942) or SS *Pilar de Larrinaga*, and the Condor cartwheeled into the Atlantic, taking its crew with it.

At the time of his death Fliegel was known to have personally sunk seven ships and damaged six more. He was posthumously promoted to Major.

Rudolf Mons

Mons was born in Vienna, Austria, in October 1914. Twenty years later he joined the Austrian Army as an Alpine infantryman, but he soon transferred to the air force. He completed his pilot training in 1937 as a Leutnant, but following Germany's occupation of Austria in March 1938 Mons found himself in the Luftwaffe. Not much is known about his flying career until spring 1940, by which time he had been posted to 2./KG 40. The Iron Cross Second Class was awarded to Mons in April 1940, followed by the First Class decoration five months later. In December 1940 he took command of the newly formed 3./KG 40.

Mons first came to prominence in January 1941, when Luftwaffe propaganda reported that he had attacked a 10,000 BRT freighter 480 km northwest of Donegal Bay on the 8th of that month. His target was the 6278 GRT *Clytoneus*, carrying general cargo from Macassar, in Mozambique, to Ellesmere Port. Mons had attacked it at 56.23N 15.28W, hitting the vessel with two bombs that left it seriously damaged. The crew of 59, plus the military personnel on board, were all forced to abandon ship. Another attack on an unspecified date saw him returning to base with 48 hits to his Condor, and he was also credited with sinking the 9956 BRT SS *Beaverbrae* on 25 March 1941 at 60.12N 09.00W while it was sailing from Liverpool to St Johns, in Canada.

Mons moved to *Stab./KG 40* in April 1941, handing command of 3./KG 40 to Oberleutnant Bernhard Jope. He was awarded the *Ritterkreuz* on 18 September 1941, by which time he had flown 51 missions and been credited with sinking 63,000 GRT of shipping and damaging vessels totalling another 32,000 GRT. Mons had also flown a number of resupply missions. Promoted to Hauptmann in November 1941, he left KG 40 for the *Reichsluftministerium*'s Technical Office as a long-range bomber specialist, after which he became responsible for the *Erprobungs und Lehrkommando* He 177 (He 177 trials unit). Promoted to Major in January 1943, Mons was given command of the He 177-equipped II./KG 40 on 25 October 1943, after which the unit moved from Burg, in Germany, to southern France to carry out anti-shipping missions.

His tenure as *Gruppenkommandeur* lasted just one month and one day.

At 0750 hrs on 26 November 1943 a Ju 88 on a long-range reconnaissance patrol reported finding a convoy off the North African coast consisting of 15 ships with an escort of four destroyers and two corvettes. There was also a single Beaufighter flying overhead. At 0850 hrs another Ju 88 reported the convoy as numbering 25 ships, one of which was a troop transporter. This aircraft also noted that, in addition to the Beaufighter, a Wellington and a number of single-engined fighters were providing air cover. During the course of the day a number of Ju 88s reported the progress of the convoy, allowing an attack to be planned. Eighteen He 111s from II./KG 26 and 15 Ju 88s from III./KG 26 took off to attack, having been preceded by 20 He 177s from II./KG 40, led by Rudolf Mons. They were to attack in the first wave using Hs 293 glide bombs, with the remaining German bombers launching a follow-up strike. This was the second such attack by He 177A-3s using what the Germans called Kehl 3, the first having occurred on 21 November 1943.

The attack took place north of Djidjelli, in Algeria, as the sun was starting to set. Of the 53 German aircraft targeting the convoy, only about half actually attacked, and 13 of those were either shot down or destroyed on landing back in France. Mons attacked between 1644 hrs and 1715 hrs with just six He 177s carrying two Hs 293s each. One He 177 reported sinking a destroyer, while a second damaged another warship. A third He 177 reported hits on a 10,000 BRT transporter and a fourth claimed to have hit a second destroyer that sank six minutes later. The fifth He 177 suffered a technical problem with the Hs 293 and the final bomber reported damaging another destroyer. The German gunners also claimed to have shot down two Mosquitoes and four Spitfires!

The Allied aircraft now intervened. Spitfires of *Groupe de Chasse* I/7 claimed a mix of aircraft, pilots misidentifying the He 177s as Fw 200s and claiming one destroyed, one probable and three damaged. Beaufighters of No 153 Sqn claimed three destroyed and two damaged. A Beaufighter of the USAAF's 414th Night Fighter Squadron claimed to have destroyed another He 177, while P-39s of the 347th FS/350th FG were credited with having damaged another Heinkel.

In fact just one ship was sunk – the 8600 GRT troopship HMT *Rohna*, which was apparently credited to Oberleutnant Hans Dochtermann of 5./KG 40. Its destruction resulted in the deaths of 1138 military personnel and crew. USAAF pilot Capt Joe Bogart was a passenger on the *Rohna*;

'I watched the action from the deck, beginning with the intensive bombing of our escorting warships and the air-to-air combat. Next, I was transfixed by what I thought was an He 177 flying at a low altitude of 2000 ft and close enough for me to see the swastika on the tail. Seconds later I saw a small aircraft below it that was streaming smoke and making a 90-degree left turn towards the convoy. At a terrific speed it flashed just above the *Rohna*'s bow, where AA fire stitched the left wing, causing it to fold, and [the aircraft hit] the sea and blew up very close to a nearby troop transport.

'I turned around to see a second small aircraft making that same 90-degree left turn, only this time it was not just heading for the *Rohna* but for me. For a second I thought it was going to hit the sea and then the nose came up and, at that moment, I thought I saw a huge hit on its

nose. It then penetrated the *Rohna*'s port side just above the waterline, blowing a huge hole there and a second hole on the starboard side.'

The only other Allied casualty was a Beaufighter of No 153 Sqn crewed by Wg Cdr Ian Stephenson and Sgt Cyril Sherbrooke, which was was seen to be shot down by He 177s. However, the losses suffered by II./KG 40 were appalling. Rudolf Mons and his crew of five failed to return, as did the crews of Hauptmann Arthur Horn (4./KG 40), Oberleutnant Fritz Noll (6./KG 40), Hauptmann Alfred Nuss (6./KG 40), Hauptmann Egon Schmidt (4./KG 40) and Oberleutnant Gerhard Strube (6./KG 40). A further two He 177s were lost landing back in France, another ditched off Montpellier and one returned with a wounded gunner. In respect of the human cost, 35 aircrew were reported missing, six were killed and eight wounded or injured. Like most of his crews lost that day, Mons still remains missing today.

Bernhard Jope

One of the best-known Condor pilots, Bernhard Jope was born in Leipzig in 1915 and had an interest in flying from an early age. He studied aircraft construction at the Danzig Technical Institute and underwent civilian pilot training at the same time. In 1935 Jope joined the Luftwaffe, eventually being posted to He 111-equipped II./KG 253 at Nordhausen, where he was the Technical Officer for the *Gruppe*. He was promoted to Oberleutnant in June 1938, and the following January saw him flying in the latter stages of the Spanish Civil War. Jope completed more than 20 missions and was awarded the Spanish Cross in Bronze with Swords.

In May 1939 he was posted to KG 76 as both the Technical Officer and an instructor, and he flew operationally in Poland. Jope was then posted to KG 28 as the *Geschwader* Technical Officer. His time with the unit was short, however, for in the summer of 1940 he was posted to the newly formed I./KG 40, joining 2. *Staffel* as a pilot and acting as the *Gruppe* Technical Officer. Jope was awarded the Iron Cross First Class in September 1940, and at the end of the following month he carried out an operation that subsequently saw him rated as a first-class Condor pilot.

Taking off from Bordeaux-Mérignac on an armed reconnaissance mission over the Atlantic at 0409 hrs on 26 October 1940, he located a 42,500 GRT liner 140 km west of the Isle of Aran at 1030 hrs. This was the *Empress of Britain*, which was being used as a troop transport. It was Britain's second-largest ship, and the tenth-largest merchant vessel in the world at that time. Jope attacked without hesitation, dropping six 250 kg bombs, two of which hit the target and killed at least 25 merchant seamen. The liner was crippled and caught fire and the Condor crew heard the SOS message being transmitted. Jope's aeroplane had been lightly damaged by flak, so, having reported what he had achieved, he turned for home. The doomed liner was taken in tow, but to no avail. The vessel's location had been transmitted to U-32, commanded by Oberleutnant zur See Hans Jenisch, who, two days later, sank the ship.

The sinking of the *Empress of Britain* was a propaganda coup for the Luftwaffe, and it was widely reported in the German press. For his achievements Jope received the *Ritterkreuz* on 30 December 1940.

In 1941 Jope flew further successful missions over the Atlantic. In April of that year he was given command of 3./KG 40, but after the second of his two brothers (Leutnant Wolfgang Jope) was killed in action on 14 August 1942, he was posted to Rechlin for service trials on the He 177. His rest from operations did not last long, as in May 1943 Jope took command of IV./KG 100 in preparation for operations in which Do 217s would carry remotely controlled glide bombs on anti-shipping missions. At the end of July 1943 Jope took command of III./KG 100 and, operating from southern France, carried out glide-bomb missions over the Mediterranean with great success. In September 1943 he was given command of KG 100, a position he held until August 1944. During this time Jope was awarded the *Eichenlaub* to the *Ritterkreuz* and promoted to Major. He then commanded KG 30 for a short time, and at war's end he was serving as a staff officer.

After the war Jope flew for *Lufthansa* for many years. He died in July 1995.

COLOUR PLATES

1

Fw 200A-0 Wk-Nr 3099 of the *FdF*, Berlin-Tempelhof, Germany, 1941

This Fw 200 started life as Focke-Wulf Flugzeugbau's ninth production aircraft and initially flew with *DLH* as D-ARHU, named *Ostmark*. In January 1939 it became Hitler's personal transport aircraft, being recoded D-2600 and then WL+2600 and renamed *Immelmann III*. In November 1939 the Condor joined *Fliegerstaffel Des Führers (FdF)* and was recoded 26+00. It remained with the *FdF*, flying Hitler and other senior Nazi dignitaries on countless occasions until it was destroyed in an air raid on 18 July 1944.

2

Fw 200C-3 Wk-Nr 0034 F8+GW of IV./KG 40 and KGzbV 200, Gumrak, USSR, January 1943

Initially called the *Ergänzungsstaffel*/KG 40, IV./KG 40 was formed in September 1941 under the command of Hauptmann Roman Dawczynski (the *Ergänzungsstaffel* forming 10./KG 40) and generally used older Condors. However, it appears that this aircraft was with 7./KG 40 on 14 July 1942 when it suffered 25 per cent damage in a taxiing accident at Bordeaux-Mérignac. Repaired and returned to service, the aeroplane was subsequently captured on 30-31 January 1943, at Gumrak in the Soviet Union, while serving with KGzbV 200 during the ill-fated attempt to resupply the German 6th Army at Stalingrad. The intact Condor (complete with hastily applied yellow eastern front markings as worn by Luftwaffe aircraft in this theatre) was put on display in Gorki Park, in Moscow, after which its German markings were overpainted with red stars.

3

Fw 200C-3 G6+FY of *Sonderstaffel Condor*, subordinate to 14./*Transportgeschwader* 4, Calato, Rhodes, Dodecanese islands, April 1945

When 3. and III./KG 40 were disbanded in October 1944, Oberleutnant Karl-Heinz Stahnke (formerly of 3./KG 40) and Oberfeldwebel Adalbert Schraffanek took two Condors to Wiener-Neustadt, from where they flew regular flights to Calato airfield on Rhodes. The Allies had become aware of these transport flights, but the precise purpose of their missions (the first being recorded by the Allies on 28 January 1945) was unknown. It was thought that they were part of preparations for an attack on the Suez Canal using Hs 293s. Normally flown by Schraffanek, G6+FY was captured together with its crew at Calato at the end of the war, G6+AY having crash-landed near Böllstein, in Germany, on 5 May 1945.

4

Fw 200C-4 F8+GT of 9./KG 40, Lecce, Italy, November 1942

On 25 October 1942 a number of Condors from III./KG 40 were rushed from Trondheim-Værnes to Lecce, in southern Italy, to support the beleaguered *Afrika Korps* in the Western Desert during the Second Battle of El Alamein. Initially commanded by Hauptmann Alfred Hemm, the Condors came under the control of *Lufttransportführer Mittelmeer* and transported fuel and equipment to Tunisia in support of Rommel's forces fighting in Egypt. Condors flew regularly to Castel Benito airport, in the Libyan port city of Tripoli, generally without incident. The detachment, now commanded by Hauptmann Rudolf Mayr, returned to Trondheim-Værnes on or around 15 February 1943. Note F8+GT's white fuselage band, this marking being applied to Axis aircraft operating in the Mediterranean theatre. Some aeroplanes also had white engine cowlings.

5

Fw 200C-4/U1 Wk-Nr 0176 GC+AE/5 of the *FdF*, Flensburg, Germany, Spring 1945

Wk-Nr 0176 was the personal aircraft of Heinrich Himmler, having accommodation for 11 passengers. The senior passenger had a private, armour-plated, compartment that faced forward on the starboard side. This compartment included a moveable sheet of armour plating that could be positioned according to the direction of the threat. It also had a personal escape window, a folding wooden table and a bookcase. Wk-Nr 0176 was captured at Flensburg at the end of the war and flown to the Royal Aircraft Establishment at Farnborough, in Hampshire, where it was given the Air Ministry Number 94. The white '5' on the tail is believed to be the *FdF* number for this aircraft, which has also been marked with the unit's eagle's head badge on the nose.

6

Fw 200C-8 F8+FR of 7./KG 40, Gotenhafen-Hexengrund, Poland, May 1944

The C-8 variant of the Fw 200 was specifically designed as a carrier for the Hs 293 missile, and, consequently, the outer engine nacelles were lengthened. Note the FuG Hohentweil aerials mounted to the aeroplane's nose and the experimental Mäander camouflage, applied from spring 1944 onwards. This aircraft was photographed at the torpedo proving ground of Gotenhafen-Hexengrund in May 1944. An Fw 200C-5/FK (FK for *Flugkörper* – rocket or projectile) coded F8+FR was found at Kiel-Holtenau at the end of the war, implying that it had replaced this C-8 when III./KG 40 was disbanded and became *Transportfliegerstaffel Condor* at the end of 1944, although some C-8s were indeed modified into C-5/FKs.

7
Fw 200C-3 Wk-Nr 0046 F8+FL (SG+KV) of 3./KG 40, Cognac, France, November 1941

This aircraft started life as F8+EL, joining I./KG 40 on 19 March 1941. On 9 July that same year it took off from Cognac at 0123 hrs to carry out an armed reconnaissance, but had to return shortly thereafter owing to a technical problem. Leutnant Robert Maly landed back at Cognac at 0244 hrs, the aircraft suffering 30 per cent damage in the process. It was subsequently recoded F8+FL and transferred to III./KG 40, with whom it was damaged in an accident at Rennes on 25 March 1942. The aeroplane, depicted here armed with SC 250 general purpose bombs and adorned with an impressive scoreboard on its rudder, was finally destroyed by German troops at Pitomik, on the eastern front, on 16 January 1943 when it was damaged yet again while serving with KGzbV 200 as part of the Stalingrad airlift.

8
Fw 200C-3 Wk-Nr 0026 F8+CH of 1./KG 40, Bordeaux-Mérignac, France, February 1941

This aircraft, armed with SD 500 fragmentation bombs, was photographed with two ship markings on the rudder, which could refer to the attack on convoy OB 274 on 16 January 1941 when Hauptmann Konrad Verlohr (1./KG 40) and Oberleutnant Bernhard Jope (2./KG 40) sank the 6256 grt *Onoba* and 4581 grt *Meandros*. Hauptmann Verlohr duly replaced Hauptmann Edmund Daser as *Staffelkapitän* of 1./KG 40 in April of that year, only to be reported missing in this aircraft during a sortie over the Atlantic on 24 July 1941.

9
Fw 200C-3/U5 Wk-Nr 0095 F8+CD (KE+LT) of *Stab* III./KG 40, Bordeaux-Mérignac, France, autumn 1942

This aircraft was regularly flown by Oberleutnant Joachim Ohm, Operations Officer of III./KG 40, during the autumn of 1942. The U5 differed in having the 20 mm MG 151/20 cannon fitted in the dorsal *A-Stand*. It was ferried from Bordeaux-Mérignac to Staaken, in Germany, on 12 January 1943 to join KGzbV 200, with whom it was assigned the code F8+DH. The aeroplane was lost on a resupply mission to Stalingrad seven days later while being flown by Oberfeldwebel Karl Grunert.

10
Fw 200C-6 Wk-Nr 0214 F8+NT (TA+MP) of 9./KG 40, Bordeaux-Mérignac, France, August 1943

This aircraft suffered a technical problem during a flight on 23 August 1943 and the pilot, Oberfeldwebel Alfred Billing, successfully ditched it, allowing himself and four crew to escape – all were later rescued. However, flight engineer Oberfeldwebel Hans Gentsch was reported lost. The observer, Unteroffizier Kurt Lelewel, was subsequently captured on 1 January 1944 after the Condor in which he was flying ditched in the North Atlantic on 28 December 1943. Billing and two crew flying with him that day were killed in action at 0429 hrs on 22 January 1944 when their He 177A-3

Wk-Nr 332231, coded 5J+ZL, of 2./KG 40 was shot down six miles south of Hastings by the No 85 Sqn Mosquito of Flg Off C K Nowell and Sgt F Randall.

11
Fw 200C-3/U2 Wk-Nr 0049 F8+FW (SG+KY) of 1./KGzbV 200, Saporoshje, USSR, January 1943

This aircraft is known to have flown with 2./KG 40 as F8+GK, after which it must have been assigned to IV./KG 40. The aeroplane was then used in the Stalingrad airlift in January 1943, where it suffered a broken fuselage while landing at Saporoshje due to being over-laden with fleeing German troops. Its pilot on this occasion, Oberfeldwebel Werner Böck, was later reported missing in action while flying Fw 200C-4 Wk-Nr 0192 of 7./KG 40, coded F8+ER (GC+SU), over the Atlantic on 24 March 1943. The reason for the loss of his Condor is unknown – four bodies from his crew were subsequently washed ashore in Spain.

12
Fw 200C-3 F8+AL of 3./KG 40, Bordeaux-Mérignac, France, 1941

The lack of Condors in 1940-41 meant that crews shared aircraft. Therefore, missions and anti-shipping successes were applied to the tails of the aircraft they were flying at the time. Photographs exist showing this particular aeroplane with nine shipping successes (25 August 1940, two on 15 September 1940, 30 October 1940, three on 6 November 1940 and two on 15 November 1940) and 28 operational flights. Later shots of it show the Condor as it is depicted here, with the codes F8+AL, an additional two anti-shipping successes and 45 operational flights. 3./KG 40 was not formed until December 1940, and according to unit records F8+AL was flown by the *Staffelkapitän*, Oberleutnant Bernhard Jope, on an uneventful operational flight from Bordeaux-Mérignac on 13 February 1941. The remainder of the crew on this mission were Leutnant Wolfgang Firsching, Feldwebels Hellmuth Schumann and Hekers and Unteroffiziers Gerhard Dörschel and Endlich. Fw 200C-3 Wk-Nr 0056, coded F8+AL (DE+OK), was reported missing over the Atlantic on 15 August 1941, although it cannot be confirmed whether this is the same aircraft featured in this profile.

13
Fw 200C-3/U9 Wk-Nr 0099 KE+IX of the *FdF*, Berlin-Tempelhof, Germany, 1942

Although photographs exist of this aircraft, its history is incomplete. Wk-Nr 0099 was assigned to the *FdF* in January 1942 and was apparently used as a support aircraft for German dignitaries on their visits away from Berlin – primarily to occupied territories in the east judging by its yellow fuselage band and wingtip flashes. Last reported in March 1945, the Condor's ultimate fate remains unknown.

14
Fw 200C-5/FK Wk-Nr 0259 TO+XO of III./KG 40, possibly Bordeaux-Mérignac, France, late 1943

From Wk-Nr 0233 onwards, Focke-Wulf switched production to the Fw 200C-8, this variant essentially being a C-5 but with a 13 mm MG 131 machine gun in the *B-Stand* and an extra 540-litre fuel tank. This particular aircraft was retrospectively equipped for Hs 293 operations and re-designated an Fw 200C-5/FK. The author's photograph of this aeroplane provides no clues as to when and where it was recorded on film, and the Condor's ultimate fate remains a mystery too. Sister aircraft TO+XQ Wk-Nr 0261 was destroyed in an accident at St Jean D'Angeley, in France, on 17 June 1944 while with 7./KG 40, however.

15
Fw 200C-2 F8+KH of 1./KG 40, Lüneburg, Germany, July 1940

Following the successful conclusion of the Norwegian campaign on 10 June 1940, I./KG 40's Condors were brought back to Germany. During the early stages of the Battle of Britain they conducted minelaying sorties around the British coast. As these missions were flown at night, water-based temporary matt black paint was applied to the Condors' undersurfaces to aide nocturnal camouflage. However, following the loss of Fw 200s commanded by Hauptmann Roman Steszyn (F8+EH) on 20 July 1940 and Hauptmann Volkmar Zenker four days later, Major Edgar Petersen, *Gruppenkommandeur* of I./KG 40, urged that Condors be removed from minelaying duties, which they fully were. It is possible that Fw 200s were similarly camouflaged for the occasional attacks on Liverpool and Birkenhead in August 1940 and Glasgow, mounted from October to December 1940.

16
Fw 200A-0 Wk-Nr 3098 NK+NM of the *FdF*, Berlin-Tempelhof, Germany, 1941

The eighth production model Condor, this aeroplane served initially with *DLH* as D-ACVH *Grenzmark*. In January 1939 it became a transport aircraft for the *Führer*, carrying the codes WL+ACVH and AC+VH before finally becoming NK+NM in November 1939. Like the other Fw 200A-0s serving with the *FdF*, Wk-Nr 3098 was fitted with an additional air intake aperture in the nose. This aircraft was destroyed in a crash-landing at Orel, in the Soviet Union, on 23 December 1941.

17
Fw 200C-3 Wk-Nr 0043 SG+KS of the Focke-Wulf Flugzeugbau, Bremen, Germany, 1940

This aircraft was well photographed both on the ground and in the air during 1939-40 whilst still assigned to the Focke-Wulf Flugzeugbau, Wk-Nr 0043 being clearly seen painted on the nose in some shots. Once assigned to I./KG 40 the Fw 200 became F8+AB, and it is presumed to have been the aircraft favoured by the *Gruppenkommandeur*, Hauptmann Fritz Fliegel. Indeed, he was shot down whilst flying it during an attack on convoy OB 346 on 18 July 1941, the Condor being hit by AA fire. He and his crew were all killed.

18
Fw 200C-1 Wk-Nr 0007 F8+EH of 1./KG 40, Lüneburg, Germany, July 1940

This aircraft, commanded by Hauptmann Roman Steszyn, *Staffelkapitän* of 1./KG 40, was shot down by AA fire while minelaying off Hartlepool on 20 July 1940. The replacement F8+EH, C-2 Wk-Nr 0023, joined I./KG 40 on 31 July 1940. Damaged in an accident on 21 September 1940, the aeroplane was subsequently destroyed in a landing accident on 21 October 1941, by which time it was flying with IV./KG 40.

19
Fw 200C-2 Wk-Nr 0016 F8+BW (NA+WI) of 12./KG 40, Orléans-Bricy, France, 1942

This veteran Condor was initially taken on charge by 1./KG 40 on 10 July 1940 and then transferred to 3./KG 40 in 1941. Later that year it moved to IV./KG 40 for crew training, where it served with 11. *Staffel* as F8+BV and with 12. *Staffel* as F8+BW. Adorned with an impressive tally of missions completed and ships sunk on its fin and rudder, respectively, Wk-Nr 0016 appears to have been a lucky aircraft, with no record of any accidents or damage. The Condor's luck finally ran out on 21 May 1944, however, when it was destroyed on the ground at the *DLH* workshops at Leipzig-Schkeuditz while undergoing maintenance.

20
Fw 200C-5/FK F8+FS of *Transportfliegerstaffel Condor*, Achmer, Germany, May 1945

On 8 May 1945 Oberfeldwebel Bergen was ordered to fly this aircraft from Trondheim-Værnes to the besieged Courland Pocket, in Latvia, but he diverted to Wuppertal, in Germany, instead, landing at Achmer. Here, he and his crew surrendered to the RAF. The Condor's national markings were overpainted with RAF roundels and the aircraft was then possibly flown by its new owners, as the Condor was reportedly seen at Melsbroek, in Belgium. The Fw 200's ultimate fate is not known, but it must have been scrapped.

21
Fw 200C-3 Wk-Nr 0034 of the NII VVS, Chalovskaya, USSR, 1943

Formerly F8+GW of IV./KG 40/KGzbV 200, this aircraft was captured at Gumrak in January 1943 (see Profile 2). Adorned with Soviet red stars, the aeroplane was evaluated by the *Nauchno-Issledovatel'skiy Institut Voyenno-Vozdooshnykh Seel* (NII VVS – Air Force Scientific Test Institute) after a brief period on display in Moscow. Its eventual fate is unknown. Several Condors were captured intact by Soviet forces after VE-Day, and at least one – given the civilian registration SSSR-N400 – was used as a transport aircraft by *Polarnaya Aviatsiya* (a division of Aeroflot) until it was written off in a forced landing at Baydaratskaya Guba on 13 December 1946.

22
Fw 200C-6 Wk-Nr 0218 F8+AD (TA+MT) of *Stab* III./KG 40, Bordeaux-Mérignac, France, August 1943

This aircraft, commanded by Oberleutnant Alfred Arzinger, was photographed taking off from Bordeaux-Mérignac on the afternoon of 15 August 1943. It was one of 21 Condors led aloft by the recently appointed *Geschwaderkommodore* and former *Gruppenkommandeur* of III./KG 40, Maj Robert Kowalewski, in an attack on convoy OS 53/KMS 23 off the coast of Portugal. Having survived this mission, Wk-Nr 0218 would be destroyed in an accident when it crashed at Malvik, near Drontheim in Norway, one day short of a year later during crew training, killing Oberleutnant Rudolf Biberger (*Gruppenadjutant*) and five crew. A solitary crewman survived, despite being severely injured.

INDEX